ASHE Higher Education Report: Volume 40, Number 4
Kelly Ward, Lisa E. Wolf-Wendel, Series Editors

Representing "U": Popular Culture, Media, and Higher Education

Pauline J. Reynolds

D1733544

Representing "U": Popular Culture, Media, and Higher Education
Pauline J. Reynolds
ASHE Higher Education Report: Volume 40, Number 4
Kelly Ward, Lisa E. Wolf-Wendel, Series Editors

Copyright © 2014 Wiley Periodicals, Inc., A Wiley Company. All rights reserved.
Reproduction or translation of any part of this work beyond that permitted by
Section 107 or 108 of the 1976 United States Copyright Act without permission of
the copyright owner is unlawful. Requests for permission or further information
should be addressed to the Permissions Department, c/o John Wiley & Sons,
Inc., 111 River St., Hoboken, NJ 07030; (201) 748-8789, fax (201) 748-6326,
www.wiley.com/go/permissions.

Cover image by © Jangeltun/iStockphoto.

ISSN 1551-6970   electronic ISSN 1554-6306   ISBN 978-1-118-96623-5

The ASHE Higher Education Report is part of the Jossey-Bass Higher and Adult
Education Series and is published six times a year by Wiley Subscription Services,
Inc., A Wiley Company, at Jossey-Bass, One Montgomery Street, Suite 1200, San
Francisco, California 94104-4594.

Individual subscription rate (in USD): $174 per year US/Can/Mex, $210 rest of
world; institutional subscription rate: $327 US, $387 Can/Mex, $438 rest of world.
Single copy rate: $29. Electronic only–all regions: $174 individual, $327
institutional; Print & Electronic–US: $192 individual, $376 institutional; Print &
Electronic–Canada/Mexico: $192 individual, $436 institutional; Print &
Electronic–Rest of World: $228 individual, $487 institutional. See the Back
Issue/Subscription Order Form in the back of this volume.

CALL FOR PROPOSALS: Prospective authors are strongly encouraged to contact
Kelly Ward (kaward@wsu.edu) or Lisa E. Wolf-Wendel (lwolf@ku.edu). See "About
the ASHE Higher Education Report Series" in the back of this volume.

Visit the Jossey-Bass Web site at **www.josseybass.com.**

The ASHE Higher Education Report is indexed in CIJE: Current Index to
Journals in Education (ERIC), Education Index/Abstracts (H.W. Wilson), ERIC
Database (Education Resources Information Center), Higher Education Abstracts
(Claremont Graduate University), IBR & IBZ: International Bibliographies of
Periodical Literature (K.G. Saur), and Resources in Education (ERIC).

Advisory Board

The ASHE Higher Education Report Series is sponsored by the Association for the Study of Higher Education (ASHE), which provides an editorial advisory board of ASHE members.

Ben Baez
Florida International University

Amy Bergerson
University of Utah

Edna Chun
University of North Carolina
Greensboro

Susan K. Gardner
University of Maine

MaryBeth Gasman
University of Pennsylvania

Karri Holley
University of Alabama

Adrianna Kezar
University of Southern California

Kevin Kinser
SUNY – Albany

Dina Maramba
Binghamton University

Robert Palmer
Binghamton University

Barbara Tobolowsky
University of Texas at Arlington

Susan Twombly
University of Kansas

Marybeth Walpole
Rowan University

Rachelle Winkle-Wagner
University of Nebraska – Lincoln

Executive Summary

From the magazines and newspapers of the mid-1800s to movies and apps of the twenty-first century, popular culture and media in the United States provide persistent and prolific representations of higher education. *Representing "U"* argues that artifacts of popular culture are pedagogic texts capable of (mis)educating viewers and consumers regarding the purpose, values, and people of higher education (Byers, 2005; Kellner, 2009). Popular culture influences consumers and viewers (Anderson et al., 2003; Tobolowksy, 2001; Ward & Friedman, 2006; Wasylkiw & Currie, 2012) and provides a vehicle for hegemonic and ideological messages (Hall, 1997; Turner, 2006; Weaver, 2009). This monograph discusses scholarship examining a diverse array of cross-media artifacts featuring higher education to reveal the pedagogical messages they contain, particularly regarding inclusion and exclusion, about postsecondary institutions and the people in them.

Representing "U" critically and interpretively reviews scholarly literature across disciplines to reveal findings related to four important foci in higher education: actual institutions, administrators, faculty, and students. The monograph emphasizes the potential to learn from and use analyses of representations of higher education in popular culture to support professional strategies, decision making, and practice. By identifying the explicit and implicit (mis)education in representations, professionals can intentionally challenge misunderstandings through programs, policies, practices, and perspectives.

The first chapter of substantive findings discusses the representation of institutions and institutional types. Institutional type is particularly salient as popular culture portrays the stratification of colleges and the people in them through select (in)visibilities that privilege or denigrate. In addition, thematic discourses position representations of higher education as separated and separating institutions, where student experience and expectations determine institutional identity.

The second substantive chapter focuses on representations of administrators in higher education. Interestingly, the focus on administrators in popular culture is relatively sparse in the literature. Overwhelmingly, the majority of administrative depictions are negative. College administrators are minimized in both artifacts and in the literature in ways that distort their role, limit who can be an administrator, and how they perform their positions. Integrity and authority manifest as key themes for administrative representations with distrust an overwhelming feature of their portrayal.

The third substantive chapter discusses representations of faculty. It develops a typology of faculty representation and considers issues of trust and power in their portrayals that dangerously misrepresent faculty work and endeavor. Ranging from bookworm to monster, loner to superstar, many of these faculty types ultimately position professors as a powerless "other" despite White, heterosexual, male professors overpopulating portrayals. The (in)visibilities of faculty of color, women faculty, and queer faculty are challenged most noticeably by female faculty but women tend to receive marginal, limited, gendered, and often sexualized representations.

The final substantive chapter assesses studies of student representation in popular culture. The chapter discusses identity and status as defining characteristics of fictional students, and the related themes of privilege and gender performance attributed to their portrayals. Separation and inclusion, alienation and belonging, and young people's next stages in life after high school are important features of the review of student portrayal.

The monograph concludes by considering four overarching themes and suggesting possibilities for the use of these themes to inform practice and perspectives within our institutions. The analysis reviews many studies and discusses many findings, but overall, the central argument is that the existing body of research on higher education in popular culture reveals a portrayal where messages about exclusivity and privilege, exclusion and omission, are dominant. These (mis)representations provide clear messages about who belongs in higher education, who belongs where, and who does not belong at all. Higher education has a deep hold on U.S. popular imagination, and this is demonstrated through the sheer volume of popular culture artifacts that include or center on the actors, institutions, and experiences of higher education. Those who come to such institutions seeking a higher education and others are likely to have developed expectations and understandings, however subconsciously, about what these institutions are all about. An important implication of this analysis is that it behooves those of us working within institutions of higher education to consider how our endeavor is portrayed in these popular culture artifacts so that, if necessary, we can take steps to help counter these portrayals and their potentially deleterious effects.

Foreword

Paper Chase. Animal House. A Different World. Community. Good Will Hunting. What do these things have in common? They all offer glimpses of higher education as depicted in movies and television shows within different time periods. Regardless of the media or the time period, popular culture shapes how people think about and judge colleges and universities. Movies like *Animal House* have left a seemingly permanent mark on the mind of society about what it means to be a college student. Obviously such movies only represent a small portion of what takes place on a college campus, but the impression can be lasting and important to consider. With massification, a broader public has access to higher education and media references are often the only source people have to learn more about higher education. In spite of the efforts of guidance counselors and well-meaning parents to inform their students and children about college, popular culture has a stronghold on societal impressions.

Pauline J. Reynolds in the monograph *Representing "U": Popular Culture, Media, and Higher Education* does an excellent job of tying the representation of higher education in popular culture to how people are informed about higher education, at times in ways that are quite narrow and limiting, as well as how popular culture can be used to provide perspectives on higher education to be educative and helpful. Media and popular culture play an important role in the beliefs people develop and the choices they make. The monograph integrates theory and related research as well as examples of higher education in popular culture to prompt thinking about the multiple ways higher education is represented to society through the media.

The monograph includes discussion of how higher education has been represented historically in popular culture as well as more contemporary perspectives. In addition to being a thought-provoking analysis on how popular culture miseducates the public about higher education (and also how it can be used to reeducate), the monograph is also a source of very interesting information about a broad array of books and movies about higher education. Readers are sure to learn more about sources of popular culture that represent higher education as well as the author's analysis of how popular culture represents the postsecondary experience. In addition to overall representation, the book includes detailed analysis of student, faculty, and administrative portrayals. Integral to the author's analysis is a critical perspective of gender, race, and culture.

Faculty who teach courses related to popular culture and contemporary issues in higher education are sure to find the monograph useful in terms of additional information about films and books that include higher education and also as a way to augment teaching and learning environments with additional resources. In addition those who do research about faculty, students, administrators, and campuses as a whole are sure to find information to provide unique perspectives related to theory and practice. Reading this book I learned much about how higher education is depicted in popular culture and also about where higher education is represented in popular culture. The monograph is a comprehensive resource for those wanting to round out their reading and watching lists.

The study of higher education in popular culture is not only interesting, but also important to the overall field of higher education. Media portrayals of colleges and universities reach broad audiences. By being more informed, scholars and teachers of higher education can introduce popular culture perspectives into teaching and research as a way to keep readers and students informed and as a means to more fully understand how people come to know higher education. The information in the monograph provides readers with the opportunity to be more savvy consumers of popular culture as it relates to higher education.

Kelly Ward
Lisa E. Wolf-Wendel
Series Editors

Contents

Published online in Wiley Online Library
(wileyonlinelibrary.com) • DOI: 10.1002/aehe.20016

Representing "U": Popular Higher Education

Introduction

ANSWERING A SURVEY SENT to incoming freshmen ahead of their new student orientation at the University of Redlands in August 2013 (University of Redlands, 2014), over half of the participating students indicated that they thought their college experience would be "much like" that portrayed in the movie *Pitch Perfect* (2012). This film focuses on rivalries between the female and male *a cappella* groups at a fictional university. Although informal and localized, the U of R survey demonstrates the core assumption of this monograph: that films, TV, best-selling novels, and other media are not merely entertainment but texts that teach viewers about things they are not familiar with, lead viewers to expect certain experiences in particular situations, and suggest ways to behave. This is a not a new perspective for scholars examining higher education in the United States. A 1920s Carnegie Foundation report attests to the longevity of this view by attributing public misperceptions concerning the importance of sport in higher education, particularly football, to the intensity of newspaper coverage (McChesney, 1989).

Numerous research documents the influence of popular culture on the behaviors, choices, and perspectives of viewers and consumers (e.g., Anderson et al., 2003, 2010; Bleakley, Hennessy, Fishbein, & Jordan, 2008; Gomillion & Giuliano, 2011; Huesmann, Moise-Titus, Podolski, & Eron, 2003;

Jernigan, Ostroff, & Ross, 2005; Russell, Russell, & Grube, 2009; Signorielli, 2010; Taylor, 2005; Villani, 2001; Ward & Friedman, 2006). Representations of higher education also influence the college expectations of high-school students (Tobolowsky, 2001) as well as college students' attitudes toward academics and partying in college (Wasylkiw & Currie, 2012). As higher education features in a large amount of popular culture, learning about the messages attributed to higher education in media is an important undertaking for those who work in or research about higher education, something that Thelin and Townsend advocated for as early as 1988 regarding college fiction and Anderson and Thelin (2009) repeated. While not a new perspective, as indicated by the 1920s Carnegie Report, this scholarly interest in popular culture and media is a minority or ignored perspective in higher education research.

This monograph interpretively surveys scholarly literature from several fields that empirically, critically, and hermeneutically examine popular culture and media featuring the people and places of U.S. higher education. Although many of the works reviewed approach the texts with questions and purposes not aligned with the interests of scholars and practitioners in the field of higher education, their findings and critical analyses nevertheless reveal insights that aid our understanding of higher education in U.S. society.

Framing Higher Education in Popular Culture

The representation of higher education in U.S. popular culture only has meaning if one makes certain assumptions regarding popular culture. For some, the words "popular culture" conjure notions of inferiority or alliances with pure entertainment. For others, the analysis of popular culture may seem an indulgent endeavor when faced with the multiplicity of questions and inquiry regarding real people and real institutions in higher education. This monograph takes the perspective that the analysis of cultural artifacts reveals a "texture of beliefs" (Surber, 1998, p. 86) or "theory of reality" (Turner, 2006, p. 133) that unconsciously influences the perspectives and choices of real people regarding real institutions and the people in them. Therefore, understanding the shared and conflicting meanings embedded in popular culture offers an opportunity for research and practice.

The perspective described by Surber and Turner is a culturalist perspective (Storey, 2012) that resonates with applications of Gramscian notions of hegemony and his subsequent influence upon pioneers in cultural studies such as Raymond Williams and Stuart Hall. For Gramsci (1971), hegemony is not static or overt but an underlying, "unconscious" facet of cultures that although dominant and covertly coercive contains within it conflict, challenge, and change. Subsequently, the hegemonic power of popular culture provides answers to questions about "What is higher education? Who goes there? What do they do there? Why is it important?" that become a vital and clandestine influence upon the negotiation of continuing discourse and action regarding higher education. As Kellner (2009) writes, artifacts of popular culture teach

> *individuals how to behave and what to think, feel, believe, fear and desire—and what not to. The media are forms of pedagogy that teach people how to be men and women. They show how to dress, look, consume; how to perceive and react to members of different social groups; and how to be popular and successful, as well as avoid failure. (p. 6)*

The field of higher education needs to take the "powerful pedagogical force" (Giroux, 2009, p. 91) of popular culture seriously. Representations of higher education teach viewers not only how to be men and women as Kellner, Giroux, and others have described but importantly for the purposes of this monograph, they learn more specifically about, or how to be, college men and women; they learn and absorb messages about the college experience and the meaning of higher education that reflect and reinforce shared or conflicting understandings.

In addition to theoretical perspectives related to popular culture, an abundance of research demonstrates the influence of popular culture media on the attitudes, behaviors, and expectations of people particularly related to violence, alcohol use, sexual behaviors, and smoking (e.g., Allen, D'Alessio, &

FIGURE 1
A Linear Model for (Mis)education

Artifact(s) ➜ exhibits norms, values, and messages ➜ absorbed by consumer/viewer ➜ contributes to ➜ (mis)education

Brezgel, 1995; Jernigan et al., 2005; Russell et al., 2009; Signorielli, 2010; Taylor, 2005; Villani, 2001). Research on the effects of popular culture uses college students as participants to determine ways in which TV and films, for example, influence the attitudes of college students toward sexual relationships (Ward, 2003) and race (Armstrong & Neuendorf, 1992), as well as cooking and food (Clifford, Anderson, Auld, & Champ, 2009). In higher education, effects-literature particularly focuses on college sports and advertising (Campbell, 2005; Campbell, Rogers, & Finney, 2007; Smith, 2008; Tobolowsky & Lowery, 2006; Yang, Roskos-Ewoldsen, Dinu, & Arpan, 2006). Other scholars note the influence of popular culture on the expectations of students and their behavioral choices within institutions of higher education, usually in ways that diminish the importance of academics (Dagaz & Harger, 2011; Tobolowsky, 2001; Tuccarione, 2007a; Wasylkiw & Currie, 2012).

Byers's (2005) concept of "(mis)education" (p. 68) encapsulates the theoretical and empirical findings of previous work, providing a crucial conceptual foundation for this monograph. She defines this concept as:

> the process by which media images concretize themselves into every-day life. It is the distance (or lack thereof) between the screen and the self, and how gender, race, class, and other axes of difference are performed through hegemonic (serving in the maintenance of the status quo) and sometimes transgressive (upsetting the status quo) televisual discourses: the ideological underpinnings that lie beneath every story and how they are put together in language. (p. 68)

"(Mis)education" influences viewers and consumers of popular culture artifacts (see Figure 1). Regarding higher education, these consumers are people who decide on funding for higher education institutions at the state level, they are people who decide whether or not Pell grants or state grant programs

FIGURE 2
A Linear Model for (Re)education

Artifacts(s) ➜ analysis reveals norm, values, and messages ➜ informs faculty, practitioners, and administrators
➜ leads to action for ➜ (re)education

should be maintained and raised, they are people who attend institutions of higher education and who work in them, and they are people who are influenced by popular culture's "ideological underpinnings" when they come to make their own conclusions about what U.S. higher education is and who it is for. As such, the power of popular culture to "(mis)educate" has a tremendous influence on our institutions.

This monograph examines the ways existing research identifies popular culture's "(mis)education" regarding higher education and takes Byers's (2005) ideas one step further. Namely, the analysis of popular culture provides higher educators opportunities to respond and adapt to this "(mis)education." When we know and understand the shared meanings represented in popular culture, we can prepare to counter and challenge their influence; we can use popular culture research to, at the risk of sounding totalitarian, *(re)educate* through our professional choices and practices (see Figure 2). Within this context the analysis of the representations of higher education becomes vital in the bid to counter the power of popular culture and support efforts to accurately project the continued relevancy of our institutions and those in them to a variety of stakeholders.

This is increasingly important in an actual higher education environment that includes rising numbers of first-generation students who have limited personal resources to seek information about engaging in higher education (Engle & Tinto, 2008; Pascarella, Pierson, Wolniak, & Terenzini, 2004; Pike & Kuh, 2005) in addition to U.S. presidential driven initiatives encouraging wider involvement in higher education to increase the education level of more U.S. citizens (Kanter, 2011). The pervasiveness of higher education in popular culture means repeated exposure to numerous messages about the value of higher education and exemplars of engagement. Even children's movies such as *Monsters University* (2013) provide exemplars of college life for aspiring college students to daydream about.

Byers's concept of "(mis)education" embraces a critical cultural perspective toward popular culture (Storey, 2012). Using a critical lens to examine the phenomenon of higher education representation in U.S. popular culture, this monograph relates it to a defining tension of higher education in U.S. society—a dialectic of inclusion and exclusion. As U.S. higher education became more accessible, visible, and possible for more people it subsequently played a more pervasive part in popular imagination and what Thelin (2011) terms our "national memory" (p. 1). However, despite the U.S.'s broad inclusivity in comparison with other countries, there still remains a tension in U.S. higher education between inclusion and exclusion where privilege significantly influences aspirations and opportunities for access and equity (Louie, 2004; McDonough, 1997; Mullen, 2010). Interestingly, the impetus for higher education related narratives in popular culture stems from contradictory but interactive extremes where both the possibility of access and the reality of limited opportunities provide a compelling rationale for broad audience interest. In this context, the who, what, and how of popular culture's representation concerning U.S. higher education plays an important part in its (mis)educative power.

Examining Popular Culture

Several key choices govern the scope of this monograph's exploration of (mis)education and the dialectic of inclusion and exclusion in the literature's analysis of popular culture's representations of higher education. This section outlines and explains significant choices and assumptions for my review including: defining popular culture and its temporal relevancy; explaining media inclusions and exclusions; and the approach to the review of existing literature. These three areas are all couched within the conceptual framework outlined in the previous section and provide ways to limit the scope of this work as well as offer a cohesive narrative about popular culture and higher education.

What Is Popular Culture?

Defining culture, popular culture, and the scholarly approaches to the analysis of popular culture texts are the subjects of numerous volumes. Repeating that work is far beyond the scope of this monograph but hopefully this following brief explanation serves to elucidate a basic understanding necessary to support my argument.

Hall (1997) states that in general, culture is about "shared meanings" distributed, reinforced, articulated, and acknowledged through language. Popular culture provides a vehicle for the distribution, reproduction, and negotiation of these meanings (Hall, 1997; Storey, 2012; Turner, 2006). Storey (2012) describes six differing definitions of popular culture: (a) simply "the liked"; (b) that which is not considered "high" culture, therefore "the inferior"; (c) mass, commercial culture; (d) culture emerging up from "the people" such as folk and working-class culture; (e) as a site to apply Gramsci's political notions of hegemonic negotiation between those with power and those without; and (f) as a postmodern perspective of blended culture without high or low distinctions (pp. 5–13).

Depending on the definition of popular culture, work in popular culture and cultural studies arguably examines "the other" through cultural, economical, political, psychoanalytical, structural, poststructural, and critical lens (Hall, 1997; Storey, 2012; Weaver, 2009). The representation of class, gender, race, and sexuality concerns cultural studies scholars with concepts such as audience gaze and spectatorship, ideology and hegemony, discourse and power, and reproduction and deconstruction, some of the means by which scholars query texts (Hall, 1997; Storey, 2012; Turner, 2006).

For this monograph, the literature reviewed examines artifacts of popular culture that align with a variety of Storey's definitions above. I have made no attempt to evaluate in this review if the cultural texts analyzed in the existing literature are popular, mass, or liked "enough" for consideration. In some ways, this indicates that my personal definition for popular culture aligns more with a postmodern description that does not sharply delineate between so-called high and low culture.

Another consideration related to the definition of popular culture for this monograph concerns historical and temporal relevancy. My research traces literature focused on cultural sources from the mid-1800s to the time of writing. The start for this time range adheres to observations that notions of popular and high culture did not exist until about this time (Storey, 2012). The broad time period illustrates a belief in the possibility of change in the portrayal of higher education across time that bears meaning. The selection of time period also parallels the manifestation and growth of artifacts of popular culture featuring higher education, supporting and tracing the idea of a unique U.S. phenomenon. Some readers might believe that any research concerning popular culture is immediately outdated but related to definitions of the popular, a book, TV show, or song may be popular in one period and completely unknown today but that does not negate the relevancy of analyzing that work to understand more about the time in which it was popular.

Media and Artifacts

The media examined in the literature reviewed as part of my research provide varied examples of popular cultural artifacts. The term media refers to the different ways that artifacts communicate their content. Table 1 delineates some examples of media type with subsequent artifacts that provide different ways of interacting with the creator's intentions.

Some artifacts generate versions in other media. For example, a popular song generates multiple sources: the printed lyrics, the musical score, audio recordings of live and studio performances, and video recordings of performances. This monograph considers literature, in this example, about the song itself, the fusion of lyrics and music rather than the performative aspects of culture. Therefore, focus remains on the previously devised and repeated, rather than immediate and unrepeatable aspects of culture.

Another important delineation regarding scope and media concerns the omission of popular culture artifacts generated by the user for this monograph. This choice excludes consideration of social media and fan fiction for example. Some readers may consider this omission to be a limitation considering the vitality and importance of social media as part of popular culture in the 21st century. However, as its name suggests, social media provides a platform for social networking and interaction; therefore, engagement in social media by users, and subsequent content, provides unmediated text(s). The format of the social media platform receives peer-review but the content by users generally does not. My research in this monograph focuses on media that has peer-review of some kind before publication/dissemination so that

TABLE 1
Examples of Media and Artifacts

Media	Examples of Artifacts
Print	Books
	Magazines
	Newspapers
	Poetry
Video/Film	TV
	Film
	Music video
	Photo
Audio	Radio
	Music
Graphic	Illustrations
	Comics
	Graphic novels
	Comic strips
	Art
Stage	Opera
	Plays
	Musical theatre
	Performance poetry
	Dance
Social	Twitter
	Facebook
	Web-page comments

the representation of higher education in these texts has been agreed upon. As well as serving as a way to limit this project and focus on products that have a formal genesis and distribution, a book involving social media would have different questions and aims due to the difference in media format, audience, and user engagement.

Critical and Interpretivist Lenses

My review analyzes literature from a wide range of disciplines including fields from the arts, humanities, sciences, and social sciences. Although broad in reach, my work is not intended to be an encyclopedic description of higher education in popular culture but a review of the existing scholarly literature. This might mean that readers find one of their favorite representations of higher education missing from mention or discussion in the text. My hope is that any "missing" artifacts will be considered an opportunity to continue examining popular culture texts in ways meaningful for the discipline and practice of higher education.

My review offers a thematic discussion of the literature derived through a qualitative-like examination of existing literature noting shared and alternative ideas concerning (mis)education within and across the literature, informed by a dialectic of inclusion and exclusion. I have supplemented my review at times in two ways: through database research of popular artifacts, and through the occasional interpretive "reading" of a text to support or add to the literature review. Examples of additional research consist of searching through the American Film Institute Catalogue and www.imdb.com for college movies or searching for descriptions of TV shows mentioned in Dalton and Linder's (2008) *Teacher TV* to determine which narratives featured professors as opposed to K–12 school teachers. I do want to note that aligned with the theoretical framework for this work, a critical cultural perspective guided by the concept of (mis)education, any interpretive readings of texts distinct from the existing literature provide just one possible interpretation of the text rather than a definitive interpretation. I offer these "readings" with the expectation that they provide opportunities for further research for those that have a different interpretation of the texts. Readers from different epistemological backgrounds may discount these interpretations as "opinion" but these readings are critical, contextualized, descriptive interpretations offered for consideration.

(Mis)educating "U"

(Mis)education and a dialectic of inclusion and exclusion focus the discussion for this interpretive review, asking: What is the popular culture university? Who are the people of higher education and what do they do? What values and beliefs are attributed to the representation of higher education? Exploring these questions, the chapters for the monograph are organized around key sites for (mis)education revealed in the analysis of the existing literature. The second chapter provides some brief historical context examining the prolific and persistent attention given to higher education in media and popular culture before the third chapter examines the setting of higher education and considers the thematic portrayal of institutions of higher education as well as the salience of institutional type. The following chapters move on to explore the people of higher education and discourse governing inclusion and exclusion as well as other features of (mis)education. The fourth chapter considers the portrayal of administrators in popular culture examining their role and characterization across media and genre. The representation of professors is the focus of the fifth chapter and illustrates numerous categories for professorial type as well as discussing the role of trust, race, and gender in professorial depiction. This is followed by a discussion about college students in the sixth chapter where student representation is shaped by the institutions they attend, their academic status, and explorations of popularity and privilege related to who belongs. All of these chapters interpretively review the existing literature, describing the possibilities for (mis)education and options for inclusion and exclusion related to popular culture portrayals. Finally, the seventh chapter discusses major themes across the chapters, considers the meaning of this work for professional practice, and the ways in which research about popular culture representation supports the work of faculty, practitioners, and administrators to anticipate situations and develop innovative proactive approaches to situations or action aligned with the (mis)education of popular culture.

From the musical *Avenue Q* to Kanye West, the comic strip *Piled Higher and Deeper* (PhD) to the comics and films of Spiderman, representations of higher education in popular culture increasingly saturate aspects of our lives. These representations provide implicit and explicit messages that influence the experience of, interaction with, expectations of, and understandings of higher education institutions, the people in them, and their roles. These portrayals (mis)educate the viewers, readers, and consumers of these texts in ways that contribute to messages about who belongs and how you belong in higher education. Understanding the messages about higher education in popular culture allows professionals to anticipate, prepare for, or work against manifestations of (mis)education regarding higher education.

Once Upon a "U": A Brief Historical Examination of Popular Higher Education

Introduction

INSTITUTIONS AND PEOPLE OF higher education feature abundantly, persistently, and increasingly in popular culture texts. Before the charter for Harvard College in 1636, early English and European literature featured the image of the professor or "learned man," including Chaucer and Brant in the 15th century, and Erasmus, Rabelais, and Shakespeare in the 16th century (Sheppard, 1990). The fascination with those who pursue intellectual endeavors crossed the Atlantic and continued in the young United States. This chapter offers a brief historical examination of higher education in popular culture demonstrating the pervasive persistence of higher education in the birth, development, and contemporary existence of a variety of U.S. media. The longevity and breadth of higher education's reach in popular culture illustrates a unique relevancy that persists as a phenomenon from the 1850s to the early 21st century.

Popular and Prolific "U": Examining Popular Culture

After Hawthorne's melodramatic but unpopular college novel *Fanshawe* (1828) (Bode, 1950), the 1800s saw a wider proliferation of higher education images, songs, stories, and discussions to capture the imagination and provide interpretations of college and college life to a wider audience. Cultural artifacts depicted the purpose and experience of higher education, and the character of those involved with it, as well as sending messages about who higher education was for (Messenger, 1981). Published in 1853, the first printed book of college songs, *Songs of Yale*, contributed to a thirst for uplifting college songs extolling the virtues of college, the characteristics of particular colleges and their students, and the pranks, events, and traditions of college life (Studwell & Schueneman, 2001; Winstead, 2005). The competitive development of rowing, football, and baseball and their inclusion in the life of college students during the mid-1800s particularly led to artistic, fictional, and media representations of college men. Drawings of college men engaged in the brutal and manly tussle of football graced *Harper's Weekly* in 1857 (Messenger, 1981), the international rowing meet between Harvard and Oxford University in 1869 caused a then unprecedented media buzz on the trans-Atlantic cable (Smith, 2001), and the allure of collegiate athletics contributed to an increasing number of fictional stories both serialized and stand-alone (Messenger, 1981). In the 1870s popular interest in college sports was such that college rowing regattas drew crowds of over 30,000 and the victors received the attention of celebrities with mass media coverage, front-page stories, and special treatment (Smith, 2001).

College women also featured in magazines, journals, and newspapers as debates considering the purpose of higher education and who it was for proliferated throughout the 19th century (Gordon, 1987; Inness, 1994; Solomon, 1985). Representations of the social life of female college students contributed to the acceptability of their attendance through a variety of articles in magazines such as regular features for the *Ladies Home Journal* including "College Girls' Larks and Pranks" and "What a Girl Does at College" (Gordon, 1987). Additionally, some fictional representations challenged conventional expectations of young women's behavior by advocating alternative options for college women including that of a more active lifestyle.

Goodloe's short story *Revenge* (1895) epitomizes these stories in a tale where a group of athletic college women seek revenge on a journalist who denigrates college women's athletic abilities and enthusiasm in his newspaper.

After inviting the journalist to their college they involve him in a sequence of strenuous activities (e.g., walking, golf, running, tennis) in which the contrast between the young women's prowess and his lack of skills demonstrates the uninformed errors of his published piece.

In addition to sports, songs, and the media battle for gender equality, a deluge of college fiction inundated the marketplace by the end of the 19th century (Inness, 1994; Messenger, 1981). Inspired by the American success of Hughes's 1861 British novel *Tom Jones at Oxford*, stories and novels featuring college highlighted the exploits of male and female students, particularly idolizing the rituals, traditions, and athletic involvement of both college women and men. These stories were penned by and for college graduates as nostalgic indulgences, while others used the medium as a vehicle to increase awareness of college opportunities, or simply took advantage of the commercial popularity of college novels (Inness, 1995; Lyons, 1962; Marchalonis, 1995; Messenger, 1981).

Around the turn of the 1900s, an abundance of U.S. higher education popular culture saturated cultural expression (Anderson & Clark, 2012). College songs, college novels, college sports, magazine stories about college students, advertising targeted at actual or aspiring college students—all prevailed (Anderson & Clark, 2012; Clark, 2010; Conklin, 2008; Hevel, 2014; Inness, 1995; Messenger, 1981; Thelin, 2011). The advent of film at the end of the 1800s also tapped into the popular excitement about college. These early offerings include short documentary-style, informational pieces about individual colleges and events, such as *Princeton University* (1897), *Yale Football Team at Practice* (1896), and *Harvard Crew* (1897), as well as featuring characters from higher education in fictional vignettes, such as the professor in *The Professor's Fall from Grace* (1898) (Conklin, 2008; Savada, 1995). Higher education's prevalent representation in a wide array of popular culture portrayed it as *the* place for young people at the end of the 19th century, a period when ideas were developed about adolescence, life course, and gender, for both men and women (Clark, 2010; Lowe, 2003).

In addition to novels, film, sports, magazines, and news media, radio programming joined the existing media in its celebration of collegiate life in the early 1900s. Radio broadcast its first college football game in 1912 and from the 1920s broadcast a variety of increasingly commercialized intercollegiate sporting competitions (McChesney, 1989; Smith, 2001). In the 1950s, radio broadcasts added a fictional series and game show to their collegiate offerings. *Halls of Ivy* (1949–1952) humorously traced the life and challenges of a small college president and his wife while *College Bowl* (1953–1955) pits college teams against one another in a competitive quiz game. Radio inspired television in the 1950s when popular *Halls of Ivy* and *College Bowl* both moved from radio to television. *Halls of Ivy* featured on TV from 1954 to 1955 and *College Bowl* retained a persistent presence from 1959. Televisual college sport also paralleled radio with its development during the 1940s. The first televised college sporting event occurred in 1939 although the technology was not developed enough to adequately display the action in the Columbia versus Princeton baseball game (Smith, 2001). From this snowy beginning a commercial giant was born.

As college themed artifacts skip from medium to medium, genre development also influences narratives. In movies, for example, plot and genre development moved from Harold Lloyd (*The Freshman*, 1925) and Buster Keaton's (*College*, 1927) freshman efforts to fit in and win the girl in silent pictures of the 1920s to late 20th- and early 21st-century multiplicity of use. The idea of fitting in and finding romance still generates plots, but these narratives now compete with horror films terrorizing sorority women, dramas exploring the midlife/career crisis of professors, the scandals and competitiveness of collegiate athletics, and comedies exploiting the experimentations of teenage freshmen, to name but a few uses (Conklin, 2008; Umphlett, 1984).

Similarly, throughout the 20th century popular music representations of college progressed from the internally generated college songs of the late 19th and early 20th centuries to expressions of sexism, exploitative hegemonic masculinity (e.g., Roth's *I Love College*, 2009), and defiant antiestablishment denials of the need for a higher education. Kayne West's *College Dropout* (2004) particularly exemplifies ideas about the conformist limitations of higher education (Au, 2005; Richardson, 2011).

College novels exclusively explored the social experiences and maturation of the students at the beginning of the 20th century until the addition of novels featuring professors and administrators throughout the 20th century expanded higher education representation in the genre known as the "academic novel." As well as moving away from solely coming of age narratives, these novels use college as a setting for satire, mystery and police procedurals, and science fiction (Williams, 2012).

Illustrating the broad appeal of higher education in popular culture, comic books and comic strips also picture college life. In the 1940s, college students in comics engaged in a variety of activities including theatrical exploits, winning football teams, and subsequent revelry (*Joe College* #1, 1949) as well as the romances of coed focused narratives (*Campus Loves* #1, 1949).[1] In more fantastic comic storylines from the 1960s, students skip classes to save cities while battling crazed professors (*Amazing Spiderman*, 1965, from #31), as well as featuring in comic strips in newspapers. College features in the 1970s in *Doonesbury* and *Tank McNamara*. Both strips develop with their characters but in the 1970s they focused on college life. Early 21st-century comics in print and online include Cham's *Piled Higher and Deeper* (from 1997), which humorously examines graduate students and their professors in STEM fields, and Willis's *The Dumbing of Age* (from 2010) set in a freshman coed residence hall at Indiana University.

Television's diverse representations moved from *Halls of Ivy*, *College Bowl*, and occasional "big games" to channels devoted to men's college sports and numerous TV narratives. The seasonal, serial nature of late 20th- and early 21st-century television follows the characters of popular high school television shows to college (e.g., *Beverly Hills 90210*, 1990–2000; *Dawson's Creek*, 1998–2003; *Buffy the Vampire Slayer*, 1997–2003; *Sabrina, the Teenage Witch*, 1996–2003) while other shows focus on professors or administrators (e.g., *The Paper Chase*, 1978–1986; *The Education of Max Bickford*, 2001–2002), but most focus on student life with professors as side characters if present at all (e.g., *Greek*, 2007–2011; *Blue Mountain State*, 2010–2011; *Felicity*, 1998–2002; *Undeclared*, 2001–2003). Many different formulaic serial TV shows mention college. In these shows stories occur each episode with a central set of characters based on a particular occupation, such as police/criminal procedural shows or family sitcoms. In police shows college provides a space for criminal activity and tragedy, while in family sitcoms children prepare for, choose, and go to college (e.g., *Life*, 2007–2009; *Roseanne*, 1998–1997;

Family Ties, 1982–1989; *The Waltons*, 1971–1981). In the 21st century, "reality" programming also uses colleges as the setting for its often sensational and voyeuristic exploration into the lives of college students adding explicit commentary on "real" college life (e.g., BET's *College Hill*, 2004–2007; *Sorority Life*, 2002; *Tommy Lee Goes to College*, 2005; MTV's *College Life*, 2009; *Quiet Campus*, 2011–2012; G4's *Campus PD*, 2009–2011).

Higher education also bears a small but increasing presence in the world of games. Thelin (2011) describes a popular Monopoly-style board game from the 1940s, "Let's Go to College," in which players must avoid academic work to progress from their freshman year to graduation to win the game (pp. 255–256). College remains even more relevant to games in general in the late 20th and 21st centuries where computer simulation and sports games use college as the backdrop for its inspiration. Simulation games such as *The Sims: University Life, Campus Life, College Girl*, and the mature-rated adult game *Leisure Suit Larry: Magnum Cum Laude* (2004), along with huge numbers of college sports games, allow players to fulfill their college life fantasies whether these involve becoming the "number 1" sorority on campus (*Campus Life*) or winning the big game. With the profusion of mobile platforms since 2010 games have also become a popular way to educate the college bound through "apps" like *Zombie College* or USC's *Mission: Admission*.

From the mid-1800s to the present topics explored in U.S. media and popular culture parallel the interests of researchers in the field of higher education. Early 21st-century U.S. movies alone manifest the following issues, to name just a few of the topics that higher education scholars examine: college admissions, choice, preparation, and access (e.g., *Admission*, 2012; *College Road Trip*, 2008; *Orange County*, 2002); college finances and the dilemmas of working students (e.g., *21*, 2008; *Fifty Pills*, 2006; *Sleeping Beauty*, 2011); student activities and societies such as Greek life and athletics (e.g., *Going Greek*, 2001; *Mighty Macs*, 2011; *Sorority Row*, 2009; *So Undercover*, 2012; *We are Marshall*, 2006); gender and higher education (e.g., *Legally Blonde*, 2001; *Sorority Boys*, 2002; *The House Bunny*, 2008; *Sydney White*, 2007); academic problems (e.g., *The Human Stain*, 2003; *Nobel Son*, 2007; *Possession*, 2002; *Proof*, 2005; *Spinning into Butter*, 2008); and faculty concerns (e.g., *Kinsey*, 2004; *A Serious Man*, 2008; *Smart People*, 2008; *Tenure*, 2008). These movies, and popular culture in general, provide numerous means to examine dominant and alternate (Polan, 1986) meanings related to topics of interest to higher education scholars.

Concluding Thoughts

This brief illustration of the distribution of higher education's representation in popular culture and media demonstrates higher education's deep hold on U.S. popular imagination, despite, or because of, its elitist legacy. Indeed, Hinton (1994) argues that, due to the prevalence of college in the national consciousness, "Movies...stand as a major part of higher education's historical record, whether we like it or not" (pp. 142–143). Thelin (2011) echoes this position through the inclusion of popular culture in his history of higher education, a strategy that illustrates the growing proliferation of higher education in the consciousness of U.S. society as evidenced in its inspiration for cultural artifacts. These representations change through time, and identifying this change holds valuable insights for faculty, administrators, and practitioners interested in the insights of popular culture higher education research (Reynolds, 2007, 2009; Reynolds & Mendez, 2012).

As demonstrated in this short descriptive history, higher education's presence in popular culture is comprehensive, persuasive, persistent, and wideranging. When we stop thinking about popular culture as only entertainment, the proliferation of narrative contact with higher education through an abundance of media and artifacts provides an overwhelming amount of data to examine concerning important topics in higher education scholarship.

Being "U": The Setting of Higher Education

Introduction

IF YOU WERE ASKED, "What is an institution of higher education?" numerous descriptive labels might come to mind. Some would be based on your own experiences, others on common, repeated messages in media and popular culture, and all would be based upon your own perspective and relationship with higher education. Existing literature examining higher education popular culture offers a variety of possible answers to this question. Some of these are interrelated, others unique, but all capture a piece of the multiple meanings attributed to cultural interpretations of the institution(s) of higher education in popular culture, exploring a higher education alliteratively beset by "deformation, divination, desecration or, arguably...damnation" (Bevan, 1990, p. 4).

This chapter examines potential meanings in popular culture related to the role, purpose, and "being" of institutions of higher education in general. It explores and interprets thematic patterns inherent in the various representations as well as those attributed to specific types of institutions such as community colleges, historically Black institutions (HBCUs), women's colleges, and four-year institutions. Perhaps unsurprisingly, higher education popular culture increasingly portrays institutions as disconnected from their actual educative purposes. The social overshadows the academic, and manifestations of institutional hierarchy viciously (mis)characterize role and purpose for institutions of higher education of differing types in ways that contain privileged messages about who institutions are for.

Being an Institution of Higher Education: Thematic Discourses

The higher education popular culture literature coalesces around four general themes when it comes to the portrayal of institutions: Apart and Away, Safe and Scary, The Next Step, and Seen Through Students' Gaze. Opportunities for (mis)education exist through interpretations of institutions as a physical entity as well as more abstract concerns related to role. These themes reveal the ways that representations contradictorily isolate institutions of higher education while simultaneously portraying them as an inevitable experience for young people. Ultimately, a challenged and changing relationship exists between institutions and the society they serve, with role and purpose represented from limited or privileged perspectives.

Apart and Away

In popular culture, literature reveals an institution of higher education as a place removed. A community in and of itself, scholars describe popular culture institutions variously as a "good place" (Kramer, 1999), a kingdom (Donahoo & Yakaboski, 2012), a religious sanctuary (Reynolds, 2009), or a place apart (Farber & Holm, 2005) in artifacts across media within various narrative contexts. Regardless of institutional type, separation and containment define popular culture institutions of higher education; they act as bubble communities with little relation to outside networks, people, or concerns, complete with unique rules, norms, roles, and behaviors (Conklin, 2008; Inness, 1995; Marchalonis, 1995; Umphlett, 1984; Yakaboski & Donahoo, 2012). Although several scholars write about the opportunities of deliberately portraying institutions of higher educations as a microcosm in fiction from the late 20th century (Bevan, 1990; Bilton, 2008), this more recent use and interpretation of the worlds of higher education in popular culture rest on the persistence of their portrayal as separate and self-contained entities.

The rhetoric of separation relates to lingering historical legacies of expressed purpose, college-building choices, and institutional development paralleling that of the nation. With the purpose of preparing young men to be leaders, the building of colleges initially occurred away from the temptations of the city, where changes in higher education mirrored evolving conceptualizations and manifestations of national identity in the colonies and then the nascent and modern United States (Lucas, 1994; Rudolph, 1962/1990; Thelin, 2011). Despite the widening of access and the move from mass to universal higher education (Trow, 1999), popular culture media and entertainment maintain an exclusive, elusive, and even incestuous portrayal of institutions that occurs across type and time periods. Higher education in popular culture reinforces that students "go away" to college, that students and professors separate themselves from home, family, and wider networks, and that institutions of higher education remain isolated from wider society rather than exist as part of it.

Across time and genre, popular culture represents institutions of higher education as places both separated and separating. The narrative choices of poems, college songs, novels, TV, and films reinforce this higher education bubble by limiting and containing the storytelling, the setting, as well as the cast of characters with campus-centric options (Conklin, 2008; Lindgren, 2005; Studwell & Schueneman, 2001; Winstead, 2005). Perspectives related to this bubble differ according to the positioning of the characters in relation to it. Those outside the bubble often perceive the boundaries of the institution as one that delineates the abstract (college) from the real (everything else), while those within the bubble rarely venture out or care about concerns outside of this higher education bubble. If they do, doubt remains as to whether they belong within this separated world (e.g., *Buffy the Vampire Slayer*, 1997–2003), or time away from campus relates to objectives with comrades from the bubble such as self-motivated quests (e.g., spring break trips and quest for the "sure thing" in the film of the same title in 1985). Venturing out of the bubble often exposes higher education characters as out of their element (e.g., a professor's awkwardness in a night club in *Vivacious Lady*, 1938, or dealing with gangsters in *Ball of Fire*, 1942), in conflict (e.g., the clash of class and racial identity between students from Mission College and townsmen at a restaurant in *School Daze*, 1987), or as outsiders themselves in higher education (e.g., Richard's alienation and desperation to belong in Tartt's *The Secret History*, 1992) (Cousins, 2005; Reynolds, 2007).

Maintaining the separation of institutions of higher education, popular culture narratives tend to focus on concerns and situations that occur on campus with characters from the campus environment (Byers, 2005; Conklin, 2008; Inness, 1995; Lyons, 1962; Marchalonis, 1995; Umphlett, 1984). Indeed, Marchino (1989) suggests that this bubble offers the perfect conditions for mystery novels as a campus "provides the ever-popular mystery format of the 'locked room' or closed circle with a limited number of suspects" (p. 92). Alternatively, Kramer (1999) describes this phenomenon as causing the "hothouse effect" (p. 9). Each description suggests pressure, tension, and conflict with no escape, the possibility of bursting the bubble.

In earlier U.S. fiction, these campus bubbles bestow characteristics or personalities upon their students (Lyons, 1962; Marchalonis, 1995; Messenger, 1981). College songs popular early in the 20th century revealed, distributed, and reinforced unique collegiate identities (Studwell & Schueneman, 2001; Thelin, 2011; Winstead, 2005). Extolled in popular culture through song and college fiction, different college identities exemplify an injustice of this separate world that bears huge repercussions for (mis)education—these worlds are presented as homogenous with little or no embrace of difference, a trait that continues on in later 20th-century popular culture (Byers, 2005; Cousins, 2005; Donahoo & Yakaboski, 2012; Yakaboski & Donahoo, 2012). However, the increasing size and diversification of U.S. higher education destabilizes distinctions between the individuality of institutions in popular culture beyond institutional type as discussed later in this chapter.

The self-contained characteristics of institutions of higher education manifested through portrayal of them as apart and away contribute to the "ivory tower" and "not real world" rhetoric littering media, popular culture, and vernacular. Ideas of separation are strong, persistent, and bear a long legacy in our cultural texts appearing in the earliest depictions of higher learning in European texts of the 16th and 17th centuries (Sheppard, 1990). As homogeneous self-contained worlds, college seems to be an idyllic refuge for students (Conklin, 2008; Donahoo & Yakaboski, 2012; Yakaboski & Donahoo, 2012), but the conditions within these worlds vary in popular culture texts in meaningful ways.

Although institutions of higher education remain a separate place in popular culture from early to contemporary portrayals, the thematic distinctions related to the type of places they depict evolve in ways that contribute to conflicting messages about higher education. Related to this theme, the portrayal of institutions of higher education as apart and away contributes to (mis)education by reducing the relationship between higher education and society to an unreciprocated, indulgent separation.

Safe and Scary

Popular culture juxtaposes notions of institutions of higher education as safe and scary in textual depictions. Genre affects the conditions of the higher education bubble explored in the previous section, as do changing attitudes toward the desirability of this portrayed state of separation. Both of these exploit safe and scary narrative choices contributing toward possibilities for (mis)education from higher education popular culture texts.

Ideas of institutions as safe or scary coexist throughout popular culture texts with the characteristics of these extremes always present but swinging more toward one extreme or the other in different genres, periods, and media. As safe institutions, the separate higher education cocoon shelters and protects the young, innocent, and vulnerable, any conflict remains mundane as narrative choices minimize opportunities for conflict (Byers, 2005; Conklin, 2008; Donahoo & Yakaboski, 2012; Yakaboski & Donahoo, 2012). The idea of campus as a sanctuary finds many guises such as providing a place of sanctuary for unwomanly women in 1940s films where female professors live out their days in safe seclusion or are rescued, if beautiful enough and able to "hide their smarts," by a man and marriage (Reynolds, 2009). As scary institutions, the separateness of institutions of higher education distorts previous ideas about sanctuary where the university is something to flee and sanctuary is only found away from campus, such as in Hoffman's campus murder mystery novels of the late 1990s and early 2000s where the university is "harsh and violent" (Hawlitschka, 2003, p. 98). Scary institutions are frightening places of protest and radicalism (Byers, 2005; Conklin, 2008; Hinton, 1994),

FIGURE 3
Safe and Scary Throughout the 20th Century

Prior to and early 20th century: **SAFE** ←→ scary

Later in the 20th century: safe   ←→ **SCARY**

that provide opportunities for evil to fester, for the ordinary to be revealed as a deceptive illusion (Hawlitschka, 2003), where features of the institution gather potential victims in convenient places for villains from within or outside to do their evil work (e.g., sorority houses) (Araujo, 2012; Archer, Stewart, Kennedy, & Lowery, 2011).

The distinction between safe and scary in cultural texts does not only rely on the appropriation and use of the higher education setting by genres that differ according to the fright factor of its subject matter. For example, early film uses characters from higher education in horror films as experts, victims, and killers, particularly the professor (Reynolds, 2007), but importantly these narratives rarely utilize the actual setting of an institution of higher education for its scary material. Bad things happen to higher education characters in these cultural texts but they usually occur off campus, maintaining the illusion of institutions as a safe place. As an example of one early horror film, *The Mummy's Hand* (1940) features an evil high priest of an ancient order as a renowned professor who goes nowhere near a campus as either killer or academic (Reynolds, 2007). However, this safe barrier around the campus gradually disintegrates throughout the 20th century with harm and terror infiltrating the safe place (see Figure 3).

Twentieth-century popular culture portrayals of institutions shift from safer to scarier places for insiders and outsiders across media from the beginning to end of the century. They increasingly become more violent and less safe in representation although notions of safe and scary remain juxtaposed in the texts and scary narratives play off the legacy of prominently safe depictions.

Events occurring within institutions of higher education and involving those within the campus community (whether it be students, professors, or administrators) increase in severity throughout the 20th century. Interestingly, the surge in darker narratives set within fictional universities parallels the increase in the diversification of higher education. For example, as more women entered coeducational institutions the conceptualization of a women's college as a "green world," an idyllic retreat for personal growth and communities of women (Lindgren, 2005), is replaced. In the 1930s, women's communities become fragmented in coeducation novels by vicious sorority silos, what Marchalonis (1995) claims is a "distortion of women's space as a place of power" (p. 126). By the end of the 20th century the amount of violence targeted at women in college movies, especially in defined "women's space," is exemplified by the fixation on sorority houses in slasher and horror films (Araujo, 2012; Archer et al., 2011).

Like the horror genre, the mystery novel explicitly contends with the projected safe/scary nature of institutions of higher education. Kramer (1999) states that within American college mysteries, institutions of higher education are not a "noble enterprise" (p. 9), despite what he terms a more "orthodox view" of this medium that claims this subgenre celebrates higher education as the "Great Good Place" (p. 8). Interestingly, in mysteries that employ this technique, such as Agatha Christie novels in which a murder occurs at a formal function or on a train, all the characters disperse after Miss Marple or Poirot solve the case. However in the campus setting everyone stays after the end other than the victim(s) and villain(s). Kramer (1999) suggests that the key to understanding campus mystery novels is embedded in this organizational feature, that the often sordid revelations about the campus cast of characters as part of the investigation reveals the flawed and decrepit nature of institutions of higher education as these awful, duplicitous "immoral and amoral obsessives and eccentrics" stay (p. 8). Relatedly, literature toward the end of the 20th century positions the university as a social institution in decline, and therefore less safe. Kramer (1999) suggests the popularity of campus mystery novels demonstrates the degeneration of institutions of higher education as the liberal arts feature strongly in these novels where they serve a nostalgic function for a threatened liberal arts education, a scary prospect.

Horror movies and mystery novels ideally exemplify the change from safe to scary throughout the 20th century, but other genres and media exhibit similar disintegration of the "great good place" through the intrusion of social and moral ills (Conklin, 2008). The contradiction of the juxtaposition of college as a safe and/or scary place gained increasing traction as a narrative strategy throughout the 20th century as the sophistication of audiences/consumers, and their tolerance and appetite for (hyper)realism, developed within different media. Ideas about higher education as safe and/or scary in popular culture subsequently act as a metaphor for the interaction of the institution with society in general.

These portrayals create clear opportunities for the (mis)education of popular culture audiences. Changing representations of institutions as scarier places could decrease the popular appeal of higher education, deter attendance, and potentially influence college choice. For traditionally aged students, the portrayal of scarier institutions provides rationales for increased parental oversight, and leads to concerns that institutions might be scarier than the "real" world beyond separated higher education.

The Next Step

Whether institutions of higher education are safe or scary, popular culture portrays universities as the next step after high school (Anderson & Clark, 2012; Tobolowsky, 2006). Readers and audiences follow the educational travails of students from high school through higher education in a number of novels and TV shows (Dalton & Linder, 2008; Ikenberry, 2005; Messenger, 1981; Tobolowsky, 2006).

Novels toward the second half of the 19th century first used this strategy. The U.S. success of a bestselling English author, Thomas Hughes, who followed *Tom Brown's School Days* (1857) with *Tom Brown's Oxford* (1861), provided a template for Gilbert Patten's publisher to suggest he write a series of boy's stories where school sporting hero, Frank Merriwell, adventures his way from school, round the world, and to Yale (Messenger, 1981). The first Frank Merriwell story was published in 1896 with other authors following this strategy including Owen Johnson who sent his popular school boy hero, Dink Stover, to Yale in *Stover at Yale* (1911) (Ikenberry, 2005; Messenger, 1981). More recently other serial texts such as comic books and contemporary fiction series for teenagers continue this strategy with the 1980s popular teen romance series, *Sweet Valley High*, moving to college in the *Sweet Valley*

University series starting in 1993 (Litton, 1996) and Peter Parker (aka Spiderman) moving from high school to university in *Amazing Spiderman* (Vol. 1. #28 and #31, 1965).

The first TV show to use this strategy was one of the earliest higher education TV narratives, *The Many Loves of Dobie Gillis* (1959–1963), where the show focuses on teenager Dobie and his friends at school before they move all together to college (Dalton & Linder, 2008). Rather than an isolated event, popular TV shows continued this strategy by sending John-Boy to college in *The Waltons* (1972–1981), following Alex, Michael J. Fox's character, to college in *Family Ties* (1982–1989), as well as featuring groups of friends journeying from local school to college in *Beverly Hills, 90210* (1990–2000), *Saved by the Bell: The College Years* (1993–1994), *Boy Meets World* (1993–2000), *Dawson's Creek* (1998–2003), *Gilmore Girls* (2000–2007), and *Veronica Mars* (2004–2007) (Dalton & Linder, 2008), as well as *Moesha* (1996–2001) and *The Parkers* (1999–2004), *Sabrina, the Teenage Witch* (1996–2003), *Buffy the Vampire Slayer* (1997–2003), and *7th Heaven* (1997–2007) (Tobolowsky, 2006).

Following young people from high school to college in narratives capitalizes on the commercial success of certain characters but in doing so (mis)educates the consumer about the inevitability of college related life choices. Ikenberry (2005) claims that college novels in the 19th century "played a crucial role in defining the college experience, projecting idealized expectations of college life to a large audience and to some extent shaping the reality of college life" (p. 53). These novels also teach that college is the next step after high school and if readers want to aspire to be like these beloved characters, they should all go there (Anderson & Clark, 2012; Ikenberry, 2005). Although this might appear to be a positive in popular culture representation of higher learning, there are two negative consequences from the portrayals of the inevitability of college attendance. First, the TV shows of the 1990s and early 2000s portray nonattendance as an embarrassing aberration, an awkward issue to be dealt with, and college as the accepted, expected next step for students graduating high school despite the disparity between high TV college attendance and much lower actual numbers of high school students who graduate and head straight to college (Tobolowsky, 2006). Second, TV and other sources of popular culture often focus on the privileged. When popular culture mainly focuses on students with resources in their narratives, higher education becomes a separate playground for the advantaged instead of an oasis of learning for all able and determined to succeed. Therefore, the next step's inevitability remains a popular culture promise that is limited to certain viewers, who remain a privileged, homogeneous group from the late 1800s to the present (Anderson & Clark, 2012; Conklin, 2008; Donahoo & Yakaboski, 2012; Yakaboski & Donahoo, 2012).

Seen Through Students' Gaze

Overwhelmingly, a dominant characteristic of popular culture institutions of higher education concerns the focus on only one of the several major constituencies involved: students. Despite the subgenre of the academic novel, which allows scholars to examine facets of academic life such as academic freedom (Tierney, 2004), or the popularity of professor adventurers in TV's *Relic Hunter* (1999–2002), Dan Brown's bestselling novels (e.g., *Da Vinci Code*, 2003), and Steven Spielberg's *Indiana Jones* blockbusters, popular culture texts and the research about them concentrate on campus life (Conklin, 2008; Umphlett, 1984) and the traditionally aged students enjoying it (Donahoo & Yakaboski, 2012; Inness, 1995; Lindgren, 2005; Marchalonis, 1995; Reynolds & Mendez, 2009, 2012; Tobolowsky, 2006; Yakaboski & Donahoo, 2012). This dominant lens bears ramifications for the portrayal of college life. Even literature examining higher education in popular culture minimizes the role of administrators, faculty, and staff focusing on student and college life experiences (Conklin, 2008; Umphlett, 1984) or limits the role of higher education faculty to only that of teacher (Dalton, 2007; Dalton & Linder, 2008). If an institution is its people, popular culture and writers about higher education cultural texts focus on the most transient but largest group, students.

Due to the prominence of the student lens, institutions are often portrayed as social institutions. Social life takes precedence over higher education's academic mission except when exams loom or professors obstruct their students in some way (Byers, 2005; Conklin, 2008; Inness, 1995; Marchalonis, 1995; Reynolds & Mendez, 2012; Tobolowsky, 2006; Yakaboski & Donahoo, 2012). Except for narratives with faculty and/or administrators as major protagonists, the work, actions, and presence of nonstudents in institutions of higher education float on the periphery, as if they are ghosts within the bubble of the separated "apart and away" institution discussed earlier in this chapter. Cultural artifacts of the 1850s to early 21st century present monolithic portrayals of students' engagement in higher education where academics are taken for granted and through students' social scene, their relationships, friendships, and romances with peers remain prime inspiration for narratives (e.g., Conklin, 2008). In doing so, popular culture persistently presents institutions as places where learning is synonymous with personal growth and life experiences instead of intellectual development relating to the majors and classes of students. Some popular culture therefore portrays higher education as an institution lacking a special place for guidance in advanced learning but as a separate place offering time-out for the privileged, without the pressures or intrusions of "real world" expectations and responsibilities.

When students' higher education is *not* portrayed as a party, a competing vision presents college as a sporting venue where passion for college sport valorizes particularly men's collegiate participation since the 1850s (Messenger, 1981). Collegiate sport in popular culture symbolizes institutional unity and community (Conklin, 2008; Messenger, 1981; Miller, 2010; Umphlett, 1984). Alternatively, narratives display institutions as selfish organizations motivated by image, competitive success, and sporting notoriety rather than care for students. This reoccurring theme manifests in early movies through the ire of Bing Crosby's professor character in *College Humor* (1933) who angrily walks away from his university position in protest over the way an athlete has been treated (Reynolds, 2007) to more recent films such as *Blue Chips* (1994) which details the bribery of student athletes. Portrayals of selfish institutions conflict with the selflessness of institutions depicted as safe refuges and sanctuary. Contested sites in the hegemonic understanding of higher education in U.S. society demonstrate ambivalence or mistrust toward institutions which can be both selfish and safe. The contextualization of the selfish institution is particularly pertinent to the student's gaze, as institutional concern with reputation and success is usually portrayed as being at students' expense.

Relationships, sports, and parties dominate student perspective narratives. The students' gaze minimizes academics and reduces institutions of higher education to consist of peers and limited pursuits. The student's gaze in numerous media (mis)educates consumers regarding the academic purpose of college and prepares future students and their parents for an experience revolving around their social lives and sports rather than preparation for and involvement in academics.

Concluding Thematic "U"

The dominant discourses revolving around institutions of higher education in popular culture focus on four thematic interpretations of "being 'U.'" Although evolving in narrative and media type, texts and artifacts from 1850s to the early 21st century portray institutions as a place reserved for privileged, homogeneous people within a separated safe place. Democratic inclusions of difference led to the infiltration of this separated place bearing greater potential to be scary. The student gaze distorts institutional existence as narratives portray institutions as offering a selective time-away before shifting in the late 1900s to symbolize an inevitable and privileged time-out. As either time-away or time-out higher education institutions are synonymous with entertainment across popular culture media; college acts as a 24-hour party and sporting venue, minimizing academic pursuits.

Being an Institution of Higher Education Too: The Salience of Type

Institutional type plays a large role in the depiction of higher education in popular culture. Repeating and alternative messages about types explicitly offer possibilities for (mis)education concerning the stratification of higher education. Existing literature veers away from commentary about the portrayals of certain institutional types such as religious and military institutions, Hispanic-serving institutions, or for-profit education, revealing embedded critique and interpretation of four-year institutions, community colleges, HBCUs, and women's colleges.

Four-Year Institutions in Popular Culture

Higher education in U.S. popular culture is typically and limitedly portrayed as a handful of like-institutions, usually "Ivy League" institutions. These elite private institutions retain a nostalgic and definitive position in the identification and representation of higher education (Anderson & Clark, 2012; Thelin, 2011). State institutions appear in some popular culture such as Fitch's "Siwash" novels in the early 1900s (Ikenberry, 2005). However, state universities usually remain anonymous and fictional in popular culture narratives unlike depictions of elite institutions. The special is named, extolled, and reinforced while the supposed ordinary remains faceless and anonymous with one institution apparently indistinguishable from another. Harvard's popularity as the setting for popular culture narratives even inspired books on how to write more authentically about the Boston university that features in numerous novels and films (Anderson & Clark, 2012; DeMoss, 2012). Needless to say, the special is also "the male" and private, while the anonymous is coeducational and public in the late 19th and early to mid-20th centuries.

The elitism of institutional choice in popular culture renditions of higher education, particularly prior to 2000, is emphasized in Hinton's (1994) examination of film from 1960 to 1990 where he claims that there is only one Hollywood film in this period that discusses junior/community college (*American Graffiti*, 1973). The visibility and notoriety of elite institutions reinforces the hierarchical distinctions of institutional type in movies of this period that not only ignore community colleges but disparage non-Ivy institutions as "second class" options (e.g., *Risky Business*, 1983). In *American Graffiti* (1973) Hinton describes the ways that graduating high school seniors discuss college going and college choice in ways that disparage and limit the contribution of community colleges. Kramer (1999) counters that in U.S. popular culture, the American campus mystery novel is far more "democratic" (p. 5) than their British counterparts that invariably focus only on Oxford or Cambridge, a situation that Taylor (1999) restrainedly comments leads to "extraordinary crime rate[s]" in these cities (p. 15).

Despite Kramer's (1999) democratic claims, elitism and the focus on elite institutions buttress higher education popular culture. A hierarchy exists and specific, oft-named institutions represent the pinnacle of higher education. Aided by its longevity, Harvard particularly shines in popular culture. Anderson and Clark (2012) note that more than any other single institution, over 100 novels focus on Harvard while numerous films and TV shows use it for a setting. Even international programming like the South Korean soap opera *Love Story at Harvard* (2004–2005) cannot resist its elitist draw (DeMoss, 2012). Unfortunately, the hierarchical nature of higher education is represented as a distinct source of "shame" for academics at four-year institutions that rank lower in this hierarchy such as Hank in Russo's (1998) *Straight Man* (Brooks Bouson, 2007).

The portrayal of four-year institutions (mis)educates consumers by relating quality to institutional history and organizational features so that exclusive higher education is portrayed as the only real higher education.

Community Colleges in Popular Culture

"Academically marginal" (p. 84) is the term used by Pittman (1999) to describe the portrayal of college night schools and programs in mystery fiction and the portrayal of community colleges across media type bears much in common with this description. If popular culture demarcates state universities through anonymity, community colleges are all but invisible (LaPaglia, 1994). A literal handful of novels appear before the 1970s (LaPaglia, 1994). As more representation occurs throughout the 1980s and early 1990s (but still totaling not much more than 50 sources in all) community college remains synonymous with "loser" in novelistic depiction (LaPaglia, 1994). Sparse cinematic portrayal also renders community colleges as "second-class" institutions at the beginning of the 21st century (Tucciarone, 2007b).

LaPaglia (1994) describes two-year colleges in fiction as "demeaning and belittling" (p. 31) and often peripheral to the narrative. Pittman (1999) elucidates that the multiple roles and identities of students not in four-year institutions limits their viability as characters in campus novels. This facet of their lives does not define community college students in fiction; it is only one of many salient identities, and usually a small contribution to their characterization. Subsequently, community college students are unable to be "away and apart" within higher education; the institution is not one that separates and cocoons the participating students. Instead, the students are themselves away and apart from the institution and this demotes community colleges.

American fiction mocks community colleges and those in them, rendering them the butt of "mean spirited images" that "demean…devalue and de-class" (LaPaglia, 1994, p. 151), where faculty are "condemned" (p. 98) to "squalid" (p. 99) and depressing institutions. Community colleges are thus portrayed as an excluded institution, barred from positive reputations and public opinion. As women are the majority of students in community college fiction (and reality) LaPaglia notes the intersection of gender with these institutional type portrayals. Intersections with race could also contribute to the negative representation of community colleges. Tobolowsky (2006) describes how smart African American student Moesha struggles in a community college chemistry class going from an "A" high school student to a working hard "C" student in *The Parkers* (1999–2004). Alternatively, this could be interpreted as a positive depiction of community college where academic standards remain high.

LaPaglia's (1994) work analyzed fiction up until 1992; after this period community college presence in popular culture widens. Homer attends and teaches at community college (*The Simpsons*), professors research meteors in *Evolution* (2001), Tom Hanks takes Julia Roberts's class in *Larry Crowne* (2011), Jay Leno jokes about community college students (Jaschik, 2005), and NBC airs a hit comedy show *Community* (2009–) set at the fictional Greendale Community College. All of these shows play with the depiction of community colleges described by LaPaglia for humorous or dramatic effect. *Community* (2009–) particularly plays with the idea of community college as a denigrated institution.

Contradicting LaPaglia and Tucciarone's work, DeGenaro (2006) and Keroes (2005) describe more positive media representations of community colleges. DeGenaro's examination of magazines in the 1920s and 1930s finds they offered little criticism of junior colleges presenting an overwhelmingly positive affirmation of the institution. Magazines during this period bolstered the growth of junior colleges through hegemonic rhetoric that extolled junior colleges as the inevitable next step in the progression of U.S. higher education. DeGenaro's work illustrates that the very aspects of community college derided in the late 20th and early 21st centuries are unique causes of pride and optimism in magazines of the 1920s and 1930s with vocational courses and more open access advocated for and valued. In an examination of more recent depiction, Keroes's (2005) interpretation of the community college in *Good Will Hunting* (1997) romanticizes the institution. Keroes interprets the community college in this film as a place that epitomizes a sense of vocation, one that used to be attached to all male professors regardless of institutional type (Reynolds, 2007). In this interpretation of the film, community college remains a church-like institution that welcomes all, not discriminating admission by class, educational talent, or purpose. Keroes's (2005) argument focuses on the ideas of "gift and commodity." From this perspective the community college becomes a place about the exchange of gifts, that professors give freely for little reward beyond the self-satisfaction of using their talents to help others rather than being governed by the need for public professional accolades. Keroes does not indicate any other popular culture texts that portray community colleges in this way so this alternative view may be limited.

Despite early press celebration of junior colleges (DeGenaro, 2006), community colleges play a peripheral, marginalized, obscure role in popular culture representation and, although gaining limited visibility since 2000, usually serve as the polar opposite of the elite schools of long-lasting visibility. Literature reveals that possibilities for (mis)education concerning community colleges particularly focus on their value and purpose in ways that diminish the talents and efforts of students, faculty, and administrators. Alternative meanings valorize the selflessness of faculty in *Good Will Hunting* (1997) (Keroes, 2005) but even these interpretations render community colleges as places for educative charity rather than personal opportunity.

Historically Black Colleges and Universities in Popular Culture

If community colleges are invisible in popular culture, historically Black colleges and universities (HBCUs) are simultaneously visible and invisible. They remain practically nonexistent in mainstream popular culture until arguably the 1980s, yet HBCUs are a persistent and prominent presence in popular culture texts designed by and for African Americans, particularly magazines.

Publications such as the long-running *Ebony* (1945–) exhibit, celebrate, and discuss African American higher education and HBCUs' traditions, rituals, and successes (Lowe, 2003; Tice, 2005, 2012). Stories about HBCUs frequently feature in the magazine, which emphasizes education as part of an aspirational strategy for African Americans in general as well as for individuals (Chambers, 2006). For example, advertisements for the United Negro College Fund and advice about getting funding regularly appear, as well as personal interest stories focusing on HBCUs: a December 1963 story reports the ingenuity of Howard University students in forming a steel drum band to pay their tuition, a July 1966 edition features Southern University's title winning track team, October 1972's cover story reads "Is the black public college dying?," while an August 1982 issue covers the aspirations of graduates from Dillard University, and annual editions celebrate Black college pageant queens. Far from invisible, HBCUs are persistently promoted and proudly celebrated in this magazine. This selective, marginal representation normalized HBCUs for the Black middle class but kept the institution hidden from wider social view.

To my knowledge, *Beware* (1946) is the first fictional film to portray an HBCU. This all-Black cast film tells the story of a struggling HBCU and the jazz-sensation alumni who saves the day, played by Louis Jordan, but the college remains high school–like in organization and structure, diminishing academic credentials of faculty and impressions of institutional quality (Reynolds, 2007). Not until the late 1980s does an HBCU serve as the setting for a TV show when popular TV and movies transcended popular culture segregation through depiction of HBCUs in *A Different World* (1987–1993) and Spike Lee's *School Daze* (1988). The opening decade of the 21st century produced several films focused on aspects of HBCU culture in *Drumline* (2002), *Stomp the Yard* (2007), and *Show Stoppers* (2008), as well as inspirational storylines creatively narrating HBCU firsts in the struggle against lasting oppressions, prejudice, and bigotry (e.g., *The Great Debaters*, 2007). For the first time since Spike Lee's *School Daze*, a college film without a historical or cultural hook identifying the HBCU as distinct from other institutions of higher education screened in 2013 (*Douglass U*).

From later 20th-century portrayals, HBCUs are contestably diverse institutions. Struggles over Black identity generate clashes between groups of students in *School Daze* (1988) (Cousins, 2005) while opinion pieces discuss the meaning of White student attendance (Crockett, 2013). Crockett Jr.'s (2013) *Washington Post* opinion piece claims, "it feels like a search for the elusive 'black experience;' through a collegiate-safari-like foray into the annals of the black history" (para. 9) asking "if the marginalized can't have the margins to themselves, then what's left?" (para. 13).

Two related TV shows offer potentially the most wide-ranging portrayal of HBCUs airing on network television—*The Cosby Show* (1984–1992) and *A Different World* (1987–1993). Parrott-Sheffer (2008) explains that *The Cosby Show* had less explicit interaction with fictional HBCU, Hillman College, in its storyline but packaged a relationship between college attendance and the Huxtable family's success through references to education, university paraphernalia, and campus visits once their daughter goes to college. He observes that others critique the show for not doing enough to promote Black identity, arguing that the token reference to university contributes toward marginalization instead of fighting against it (Parrott-Sheffer, 2008). However, Parrott-Sheffer finds *A Different World* provides a vital contribution to HBCU portrayals on TV, presenting a warm, supportive college environment. This successful mainstream show appealed to viewers and portrayed an exemplar of the HBCU world.

In contrast to the nurturing HBCU environment envisioned in TV fictional narratives, newspapers and reality TV programming present more challenging representations of HBCUs. In her analysis of media coverage surrounding Morris Brown College in 2002–2003, Gasman (2007) reveals that issues faced by this one institution become a rhetoric of decline for all HBCUs where news stories go beyond questioning the value and purpose of HBCUs to worryingly negating them. Additionally, producers designed the reality TV show *College Hill* (2007–2011) with the purpose of focusing on difference, of portraying the uniqueness of HBCU culture. However, the result is highly sensational narratives with students artificially thrown together to cause optimum conflict and controversy (Parrott-Sheffer, 2008).

HBCUs remain separated through racial and cultural differences from other portrayals of institutions of higher education yet they are also portrayed as differentiated within, perhaps more so than the homogeneous portrayals of institutions of higher education in general. The intersection of race with institutional type remains important for portrayals of HBCUs. Despite the negativity Parrott-Sheffer discerns in *College Hill's* "real" narratives he reveals that enrollments increased after the show aired and that the damage to HBCUs may have been worse if it had aired on a channel other than BET.

With simultaneously (in)visible representation, HBCUs in popular culture portray segregated relevancy for consumers. Possibilities for (mis)education revolve around the significance and worth of HBCUs differentiated by an audience which potentially devalues the broad importance of minority-serving institutions as a whole.

Women's Colleges in Popular Culture

Akin to HBCUs, selective visibility in different periods impedes consistency of presence for women's colleges in popular higher education. Unlike HBCUs which gained more presence at the end of the 20th century, the opposite occurs for the visibility of women's colleges, which aligns in many ways to the fortunes of actual institutions. Writers penned numerous stories about women's colleges at the turn of the 1900s (Inness, 1995) but in the 21st century depictions are limited to the occasional film (e.g., *Mona Lisa Smile*, 2000; *Mighty Macs*, 2011) or references to women's colleges that position them as scary fortresses of feminism (e.g., *10 Things I Hate About You*, 1999). References exist in popular culture about specific characters being Smith or Vassar graduates, for example, and characters in the web comic *Questionable Content* work in the library and take classes at "Smif" (Smith College, #691). Yet little early 21st-century popular culture uses the narrative setting of women's colleges.

Girls' fiction featured women's colleges strongly around the turn of the 1900s and presented the single-sex institution as one that would liberate women with previously unknown freedoms and activities yet appease

---

worried parents with rules and a separated setting (Inness, 1995). Dispelling fears about women's education and "race suicide," an excitable concern of the late 19th century (Solomon, 1985), novels of the Progressive Era position women's colleges as a place of community, serving to prepare women for their gendered roles in society as mothers and wives through their hierarchical and structured relationships with other female peers (Inness, 1994, 1995; Lindgren, 2005; Marchalonis, 1995).

Marchalonis's (1995) examination of college women's fiction describes how college novels before 1900 extol women's colleges as a place for women to find community and space in "the green world" (p. 25). Marchalonis concedes that space is also important in the men's college novels of the time; however in the men's novels "young men roam" (p. 26) while the young women enter a contained space of idyllic retreat. Instead of a separate sphere, indeed engaging in an activity that for many contemporaries threatened the very idea of separate spheres of influence for the sexes, college women's novels introduce their characters and readers to a separate space where young women had a defined period to finish their girlhood. College women at this time were termed "college girls" as leaving college signaled their entrée into womanhood and subsequent expectations (Marchalonis, 1995).

The dark side of this idyllic retreat relates to the structural and organizational attempts to control and contain. Women's college novels of the Progressive Era portray institutions seeking to control their students, balancing the management of external fears related to masculinization and race suicide with notions of femininity and appropriate academic engagement (Inness, 1995). In fact, Inness (1995) notes the resemblance in rhetoric and choices between women's colleges and prisons during the Progressive Era especially concerning domestic and disciplinary "space" (p. 20).

Contradictorily, despite the attempts to control female students, women's colleges provide a way to find individual voice through community participation and identification. Inness (1993) posits that through engagement in athletics, either as a player or spectator, these fictional college women used opportunities, freedoms, and restrictions at their women's colleges as a way to "rebel against the social ideology that considered women's bodies little more than baby machines" (Inness, 1993, p. 118).

As women's fiction develops in the early 20th century, women's colleges become less a separate sphere but more of a "roundabout." Rather than staying put in their wonderful retreat the outside world impinges more and more on the stories bringing adventures, car trips, and, consistent with heteronormative narratives, welcome male visitors (Marchalonis, 1995).

Films from the 1940s reinforce the separation of women's colleges as a barred world. A swimming instructor in *Bathing Beauty* (1944) hides away in a women's college to avoid the attentions of a boyfriend she believes betrayed her (Reynolds, 2009). Yet this and other narratives subvert the barrier and "penetrate" women's safe seclusion as students sneak out or men sneak in. Red Skelton uses a legal loophole in *Bathing Beauty* (1944) to get admitted to the women's college to pursue his love interest, while students sneak out of Smith College to elope in *Rich and Famous* (1981) (Conklin, 2008; Reynolds, 2007). In 2013, the idea of infiltration and self-contained women's colleges inspired Tina Fey to develop a comedy about a fictional women's college that opens its doors to men. The premise for this show was so hot that a bidding war for rights ensued between networks (Andreeva, 2013). Although the announcement of this show challenges the appearance of the decreased relevancy of women's college in 21st-century popular culture, its premise actually reinforces this argument as it is men's inclusion in this college that generates comedic opportunities and makes the show one that has value for a contemporary audience (Goldberg, 2014).

Popular culture texts using women's colleges evolve from celebration and censure to comparative irrelevancy from the late 1800s to the 21st century. The respective decreasing and increasing of portrayals for women's college and HBCUs is an interesting observation if one equates the prevalence of portrayal with the cultural relevancy of these actual institutional types. It is also fascinating that the two movies featuring women's colleges in the 21st century are historical portrayals while HBCU depiction is so current, so today, that it epitomizes one of contemporary TV's "realities." Popular culture (mis)educates consumers regarding the use and value of women's colleges, particularly in the 21st century. Women's colleges transform from a necessary and contested institution in the late 1800s to an unnecessary and irrelevant institution in the 21st century. Their portrayal renders them an institution of the past rather than one of the present, something that existing women's colleges would dispute in the 21st century, but that the decreasing numbers of actual institutions would support.

Concluding Thoughts

From the earliest depictions of institutions of higher education contradictions exist in the various projections of the "being" of institutions of higher education that cause tensions, ambiguities, and possibilities for (mis)education. In this examination of the literature, popular culture negotiates the value, reputation, and worth of institutions. Popular higher education exaggerates the features and roles of institutional types to reinforce notions of hierarchy and relevancy. Elite institutions receive repeated free marketing extolling their excellence and exclusivity while other institutions' worth is diminished.

Institutional representations clearly exhibit, reinforce, and challenge ideas about privilege related to type that projects messages about who belongs. Interestingly, these portrayals also change in ways that indicate further scrutiny is necessary. Complexity, contradiction, and change characterize the collective representations from 1850 to the 21st century. Separate yet infiltrated, safe yet scary, elite and mediocre, selfish and selfless, visible and invisible, portrayals of institutions provide limiting options that are stratified according to projections of worth that fail to sophisticatedly offer possibilities for inclusion. Beyond institutional portrayals, the analysis of the people who work in and use these fictional institutions adds to the potential for (mis)education revealed in this chapter. The following chapter explores the portrayal of the administrators who run these contradictory institutions.

Running "U": Administrators in Popular Culture

Introduction

DESPITE THE INCREASING PRESENCE of administrators across U.S. institutions of higher education throughout the 20th century, they are minimally represented as major protagonists in popular culture. Therefore, limited scholarly literature considers college administrators in popular culture and only a handful focus specifically on their representations. Akin to actual demographics since higher education's beginnings in America, popular culture administrators, until more recent depictions, are usually older White men representing roles such as presidents, deans, registrars, advisors, and admissions officers. Administrators deal with the same issues as their actual counterparts fielding problems and complaints initiated by student and faculty behavior as well as academic problems related to finances, curriculum, academic freedom, hiring and promotion, and personnel (Crowley, 1994; Pittman & Theilmann, 1986). This chapter explores the popular culture administrator through a descriptive examination of their characterizations as well as a thematic perspective that considers attributes allied with role. Opportunities for (mis)education increase through the ways administrators are presented but also through their absence or remoteness in popular culture.

Being a Higher Education Administrator: Types and Presence

Although rarely examined in scholarly work, a variety of positions feature in popular culture particularly in more recent narratives. Academic deans, the president, and the dean of students, the latter played by Sarah Jessica Parker, discuss how to tackle racism on campus in *Spinning into Butter* (2008). Other deans of students welcome students to their campuses in *Monsters University* (2013) and *Community* (2009–), or futilely fight against Greek institutions as "The Dean" in *Animal House* (1978), *Revenge of the Nerds* (1984), and similar movies (Conklin, 2008). An admissions team conducts school recruitment visits and discusses the merits of applicants in *Admission* (2013), while other admissions officers feature in *P.S.* (2004) and *Orange County* (2002). Finally, academic advisors guide students in *Felicity* (1998–2002), *Greek* (2007–2011), and the online comic strip *Alternate University* (2010–).

Narratives use the actual responsibilities of administrators to guide their involvement in plots and describe their involvement in the routine of their jobs as incompetent, indifferent, or superb exemplars of their role (Pittman & Theilmann, 1986). Authors and producers also use the social contexts of the times they write about and in to explore intrinsic and extrinsic issues, for example, student determinism, McCarthyism and academic freedom, and Vietnam and student protest (Conklin, 2008; Crowley, 1994; Hinton, 1994; Kramer, 1981, 1999; Pittman & Theilmann, 1986). Several scholars declare that as popular culture texts tend to be written by former students and faculty members who may have been restricted by administrators in some way, interpretations of popular culture portrayals report a generally negative representation of administrators across media type dominated by ideas related to authority and integrity (Bevan, 1990; Conklin, 2008; Hinton, 1994; Kramer, 1981, 1999; Pittman & Theilmann, 1986; Tobolowsky, 2006).

Depending on the media, genre, and plot, administrative characters range from completely invisible in college narratives (Tobolowsky, 2006) to major protagonists (Kramer, 1981; Pittman & Theilmann, 1986). Tobolowsky (2006) suggests their invisibility in teen TV college fictions (mis)educates viewers about the role of administrators in higher education and of their appropriateness as avenues for student support. Invisibility is not the only cause for concern related to college administrators in popular culture. When they do appear they are seldom depicted positively. As Kramer (1999) claims, "most American college mysteries are testimonies to inadequate administration" (p. 12), and administrators fuel the context for the genre's murders through mismanagement, apathy, absence, or "active participation" (p. 9).

Presidents and deans bear the brunt of fictional negativity. Although popular culture first portrayed warm, benevolent leaders in Hawthorne's *Fanshawe* (1828) and radio (1949–1952) and then TV's (1954–1955) *Halls of Ivy*, trust swiftly becomes a problem in representations across media. Describing university fiction, Bevan (1990) claims, "Presidents and vice-chancellors are almost uniformly vain, ambitious, aggressive, ruthless and haughty" (p. 105). More than 20 years after *Halls of Ivy* a college president returns to the small screen in *Hanging In* (1979–1979). However, this portrayal is more reminiscent of presidential depiction in the movie *Horse Feathers* (1932) than the *Halls of Ivy*'s kindly president as it follows a professional footballer that becomes a university president upon his sporting retirement (Dalton & Linder, 2008). It seems a college president can be anyone on TV, or rather, any White male. Interestingly, it is not until over 20 years after a retired professional footballer is president that a female president of a university is depicted on TV in *The Education of Max Bickford* (2001–2002).

Although male dominated in popular culture and reality, women appear as presidents in Walworth's novel *Feast of Reason* (1941), the film *PCU* (1994), as well as TV's *The Education of Max Bickford* (2001–2002) (Conklin, 2008; Dalton & Linder, 2008; Kramer, 1981). Rather than indicating acceptance of women in these leadership roles their placement in institutional types and plot choices arguably support male administrative superiority. *The Education of Max Bickford* shows an African American woman as the president of a women's college. Making tough decisions that affect her friends, she is the only president not to lose her job in these examples but her influence is contained to that of female students within a women's college, her authority limited to women's space. Hollywood's college president in *PCU* is fired after her failure to "control" students, potentially suggesting that her hiring in the first place was a concession to the political correctness the film sends up instead of her credentials. And finally, Walworth's president in *Feast of Reason* presides over a junior college, which, as the third chapter illustrates, designates it as an inferior institution, but even within this so-portrayed "lowly" institution she cannot succeed. She tries to use her power to seduce and coerce an instructor into a relationship with her. When this fails to succeed she retaliates against the instructor and his love interest before losing her position (Conklin, 2008; Dalton & Linder, 2008; Kramer, 1981).

Other female administrators in popular culture are presented as flawed. Sarah Jessica Parker plays a dean of students who struggles with her own racism, something her character confronts after a spate of racial incidents on campus in *Spinning into Butter* (2008), and a female graduate college admissions administrator, played by Laura Linney, seduces a prospective student in *P.S.* (2004). It is unfortunate that the sparse portrayal of women leaders in popular culture (mis)educates viewers/consumers by presenting them as incompetent, exhibiting poor sexual judgment in the work place, acting vindictively, or as limited in sphere.

Although barely visible en masse in popular culture, literature suggests that these select portrayals minimize college administrators, distort their role, and limit who can be an administrator and how they perform their positions. (Mis)education occurs related to the presence and importance of these positions.

Being a Higher Education Administrator: Thematic Discourses

Two major and interrelated themes shape the representation of administrators in popular culture. Moving from benign beginnings in fiction and radio to negative or invisible roles in certain popular culture media, the negativity takes advantage of administrative power to question and undermine the integrity and authority of administrators in various roles, contributing toward possibilities for (mis)education about administrators.

Integrity and Its Compromise

Administrators in popular culture such as presidents and deans wear the lonely mantle of power that separates them from others in the university community. Presidents particularly act as figureheads for the scholarly community, rarely interacting with students. Kramer (1981) points out that presidents seldom interact with students particularly in pre-Vietnam Era novels. Linn's *Winds over Campus* (1936) provides an example of presidential remoteness when the president tells the new students gathered at orientation to "take a good look at me now because you will probably not see me again until the day of your graduation" (Kramer, 1981, p. 89, footnote).

Moralizing in earlier popular culture texts complements this remoteness. The "saintliness" of presidential clergyman Reverend Dr. Melmoth in Hawthorne's *Fanshawe* (1828) (Kramer, 1981) is followed by morality laden presidential speeches in films of the 1930s, extolling campuses as family communities with the members of the community bearing responsibilities and duties (Conklin, 2008). As saintly figures the heteronormative narratives portray presidents as faithfully married or morally alone. Kramer (1981) finds the epitome of these characteristics in the aptly named "President Avery Monck" in Ballard's *The Man who Stole a University* (1967) where the president demonstrates his "very monkly" moral core by not taking advantage of a naked female student awaiting him in his bed. However, punishment awaits gay presidents or those with narratively deemed weaker moral compasses who cheat on their wives or try to sleep with students or faculty. Narrative sentences include the threat of castration and banishment (Cassill's *The President*, 1964), loss of employment (Walworth's *Feast of Reason*, 1941), and death (Hoyt's *Wings of Wax*, 1929) (Kramer, 1981). In a surprising twist, narratives also punish presidents who defend academic freedom such as the president who loses his job in Kubly's *The Whistling Zone* (1963) (Kramer, 1981). Therefore, presidents are punished by compromising their personal integrity and by failing to compromise their professional integrity in these popular culture texts.

Displays of vanity and ambition dissolve the integrity of fictional presidents in novels (Kramer, 1981). Kramer (1981) alliteratively states, "fictive presidents preen themselves when in private and posture when in public"

(p. 82) in describing the vanity that abounds in presidential depictions. Fictional presidents fuel their ambitions by undermining academic freedom (Kramer, 1981) and academic standards (Conklin, 2008), apparently being willing to become "politicians" and say what people want to hear to resolve problems (Hinton, 1994, p. 112).

Athletics receives particular attention in narratives as a source for the dissolution of administrative integrity. Texts illustrate administrators compromising academic standards in the hope of athletic success, pressuring professors to pass struggling students so they remain eligible to play in the "big game," and outmaneuvering faculty in administrative efforts to put sporting success ahead of academics (Conklin, 2008). Through these efforts administrators actualize the selfish institution described in the third chapter, where institutional reputation, demonstrated through sporting prowess, is more important than students' learning or institutional academic standards. Administrators make choices in these narratives to gamble on short-term gains and take the credit for any subsequent success to fuel advancement. As Hinton (1994) writes, "College administrators are cold-hearted, unscrupulous individuals interested only in raising money for the college, protecting its image, and undermining student individuality" (p. 159). Alternatively, *R.P.M.: Revolutions per Minute* (1970) provides an interesting examination of integrity focused on the office of president. This movie centers on campus unrest at the end of the 1960s. A beleaguered president resigns amid the turmoil and the students insist that a sociology professor who supports activism take his place. The new president becomes caught between his support of students and his need to preserve the university (Conklin, 2008; Hinton, 1994).

The analysis of popular culture texts reveals dual roles for the integrity of administrators where morality, good intentions, and paternal pastoralism are demolished by the individual ambitions of administrators leading to the manifestation of the selfish university through the choices and behaviors of institutional leaders.

Authority and Its Abuse

Authority is all about the use of control in popular culture narratives. Administrators sometimes act as literal or metaphorical generals or "enforcers" in film to curb protest, restrain unruly student groups, and limit student voice (Conklin, 2008; Hinton, 1994). They watch, restrain, and police against antifeminine behaviors (Inness, 1995), and "subversive" relationships with other women in women's fiction (Inness, 1995; Marchalonis, 1995). They also act as academic gatekeepers for women at coeducational institutions, limiting women's proliferation of their academic sphere to "women's courses" instead of catering to their interests and abilities (Marchalonis, 1995). As institutional leaders who often stand for maintaining acceptable limits for student behavior in popular culture, administrators act as a foil for the demonstration of students' independence that increases from the late 1800s to the 21st century.

Administrators are often villains, incompetent, or both, being authority figures to rebel against or dismiss. Tucciarone (2007a) claims their presence and actions provide justification for student demonstrations of "rebellion or retaliation" (p. 853) in popular culture narratives, particularly in those akin to *National Lampoon's Animal House*'s (1978) portrayal of the nefarious Dean Wormer. Movies like *Animal House, Revenge of the Nerds* (1984), and *Old School* (2003) position administrators as enemies who must be bested, and the fictional administrators actively engage in this battle (Conklin, 2008). Interestingly, earlier depictions of popular culture rarely waste time on administrative positions and their influence on student life. Partly this is due to the small number of actual administrators and staff but conflict and competition rested between student classes in popular culture texts, as discussed later in this monograph in the exploration of "Being a Student," instead of between students and administrators. In some ways the shift to incompetent administrators taps into different manifestations of teen insularity where students know better than the adult administrators attempting to manage or curtail their social activities who are portrayed as abusing power and bested by students who have less organizational power but more imaginative, smart, and charismatic power.

To exhibit control administrators engage in a variety of behaviors, many of which are not exemplars for actual administrators. Extreme examples in popular culture include one institution's simultaneous use of the National Guard, Air Force, and paratroopers to quell student unrest (Pittman & Theilmann, 1986), while another embraces public execution (Kramer, 1981). Walton displays the latter instance of administrative control in the novel *No Transfer* (1967) where the only way to leave the institution alive is to graduate. Struggling students are encouraged to be more diligent through the public execution of one of the weaker students three times a year at the hands of one of the successful students (Kramer, 1981). The president significantly boosts retention of the student body and the success of those enrolled with this strategy. Apparently, the guillotine bears huge success at encouraging students' academic motivation.

Conklin (2008) identifies a Hollywood tension between administration and Greek life that is examined and exploited in numerous movie texts. Since *Animal House* (1978), Greek houses are the first suspects for pranks on campus and often engage in battles with deans who they blackmail and get fired in the movies (Conklin, 2008). The administrators in these examples always display leadership inadequacies and incompetence in their dealings with the Greek system. Conklin suggests that these depictions even (mis)educate the actual disposition of administrators and faculty toward Greek life, with administrators becoming "more hostile" to Greek life since *Animal House* initiated this type of storyline. This theme also jumps medium and becomes the focus for major storylines on TV in *Delta House* (1979) and *Greek* (2007–2011) (Dalton & Linder, 2008; Reynolds & Mendez, 2009, 2012).

Administrators use and misuse their authority in these texts in ways that mistreat specific student groups and set themselves up as even more of a target for rebellion and as objects for student determinism.

(Mis)running "U"?

Being an administrator in popular culture presents a role initially ignored in texts bar the occasional depiction of a president or dean, to fuller explorations of these roles during the 20th century, and then 21st-century depiction of administrators beyond these roles. Administrators have not been major protagonists in a host of texts and many roles stereotype rather than complexly explore their roles and relationships within the campus community yet the distrust associated with many of the negative portrayals across media type bears the potential for (mis)education in ways that can alter the perspectives, perceptions, and interactions of actual students with administrators and vice versa (Conklin, 2008; Tobolowsky, 2006). In fact, the analyses of texts suggest that administrators "mis-run," neglect, and use the institutions they serve. Groups of students are singled out for the attention of administrators—athletes, Greeks, and protestors—and administrators use their authority to control students and compromise their integrity to manipulate students in narratives. Possibilities for (mis)education include knowledge about the roles and responsibilities of administrators which is limited, lacking, or distorted in popular culture texts.

Professing "U": Faculty in Popular Culture

Introduction

SINCE THE 15TH CENTURY, Western literature features professors as "the learned," or as "comic fools," "damnable fools," "frauds and depraved rogues," and "damnable or diabolic (quasi-) magicians" (Sheppard, 1990, p. 12). Professorial depiction persists and increases cross-media from these roots where the gender, race, sexuality, class, disciplines, work, and behaviors of faculty provide multiple opportunities for (mis)education. Popular culture's depiction of professorial role and characteristics has the potential to (mis)educate in three main ways: the reception of actual professors in the academy, how students interact with professors, and how other viewers/consumers understand their work and role (Dagaz & Harger, 2011; Tobolowsky, 2001; Tucciarone, 2007a, 2007b). This examination of the professor in popular culture focuses on related areas of representation: categorizing the depiction of popular culture professors; exploring trust and the professoriate; the White, straight, male status quo; and the gendered challenge. Literature about professors as one participant in the cast of higher education uses choices about how to present professorial work and worth, juxtaposing ideas about inclusion and exclusion in the portrayal of the profession.

Categorizing Popular Culture Professors

The literature examined for this monograph implicitly and explicitly expresses descriptions and commentary on a variety of professorial types revealed across popular culture media. The depiction of faculty depends on the positioning of the major protagonist and their interaction with professorial characters, revealing stereotypes and themes both familiar and more novel. Although some of these types portray professors positively, often these characterizations are deficit-based with the professors lacking something (e.g., practicality, social skills, or love). The manner of their deficit often results from the different lens used to position faculty in popular culture. In my analysis of the literature, I identify these lenses as defined by the students' gaze, colleagues' gaze, or a nonacademic gaze. As shown in Table 2, the nonacademic gaze toward professors is particularly harsh exhibiting only two potentially positive types, "the genius" and "the hero." Perceptions of deficit relate to the nature, worth, and understanding of professorial work that impacts the trust associated with faculty.

Examples of these professorial types, and perhaps others omitted here, can be found across popular culture representations of professors. Lyons (1962) claims that the roots for American absent-minded professors began with Hawthorne's *Fanshawe* (1828) while other early fiction renders professors invisible as in Johnson's *Stover at Yale* (1911), for example. Nicol (2011) describes the professor in *Arlington Road* (1999) as a "lone maniac" (p. 205) alienated by his obsessive, but correct, suspicions of his neighbors' criminal activities. Using a professor as protagonist in *Arlington Road* allows the professor's expertise to add to the validity of his claims but the choice of a professor may additionally contribute to the disbelief and distrust others give him as he steps outside of the separate world of higher education, as discussed in the third chapter, and tries to expose his neighbors.

Discipline also influences depictions of professorial types, magnifying or minimizing the gazed perspective. Ambivalence and fear dominate the representation of scientists, particularly chemists, in popular culture (Ball, 2006; Gerbner, 1987; Haynes, 2003, 2006; Terzian & Grunzke, 2007; Weingart, 2006). Indeed, professorial villains are ably represented by the mad scientist

TABLE 2
Typology of Professors in Popular Culture

The Gaze	Professorial Type	Description
Nonacademic Gaze	The Loner	The solitary nature of some scholarly pursuits separates professors from others. Work becomes a barrier.
	The Bookworm	Alliance with books, research, and lack of physical activity leads to this usually derogative label.
	The Indolent	Perceived as an inactive, idle, nonworker, and doing little of use as it can't generally be seen or understood and therefore without respect.
	The Absent-Minded Genius	Distracted, at times impractical, accident prone, not part of the real world. Brilliant and unique.
	The Lecherous	Sexually preys on members of the campus community, usually students.
	The Villain	Including depictions of the "mad scientist," these professors are evil masterminds motivated by the acquisition of power and wealth far beyond that garnered through academic work. Could be evil geniuses corrupted by their intellect.
	The Monster	Professors metaphorically and literally represented as monsters, vampires, ghouls, mummies, and beasts that prey on those inside and outside the academic community.
	The Tolerated/ Unimportant Necessity	Barely present and inconsequential to student experience and college life.
	The Hero	Despite or due to scholarly expertise, the professor wins the girl, beats the bad guys, or saves the world.

(Continued)

TABLE 2
Continued

The Gaze	Professorial Type	Description
Student Gaze	The Lover/Husband/ Partner	Advances usually made by others to initiate relationships or a relationship or marriage already exist. Due to male privilege and the representation of the professoriate, the use of "husband" is deliberate.
	The Lecherous	Sexually preys on members of the campus community, usually students. Or married professors who have affairs.
	The Enemy	Impedes student progress, a barrier to be fought through, and a gatekeeper for success.
	The Teacher/Mentor	An inspiration and guide.
	The Scholar	Depending on the type of student, an admired or terrifying professor.
Academic Gaze	The Deadwood	Noncontributor to department or scholarship. Regurgitates the same courses again and again with no new materials or innovations.
	The Annoyance	Challengers to, or enforcers of, the status quo. Could be sexual harassers, feminists, or someone with pet peeves or axes to grind.
	The Faker	Acting the role of professor, faking discipline expertise, all surface, no substance.
	The Superstar	The globe trotting, brilliant, publishing machine, who inspires students and can do no wrong.

stereotypes who scare through their attempts to achieve God-like powers, break or transcend known limits, master and own "forbidden knowledge," and create monstrous machines or new life (Hark, 2004; Toumey, 1992).

Other fields also amplify the effectiveness of types. Archeologists represent higher education's heroes where adventure, quests, digging, and discovery characterize their depiction (Day, 1997; Hall, 2004; Holtorf, 2007; Membury, 2002). Alternatively, the portrayal of sociologists renders them as enemies or unimportant necessities through depictions of ridiculous, impractical procedures and professional denigration where they are accused of observing instead of engaging, and analyzing instead of feeling and reacting (Bjorklund, 2001; Kramer, 1979; Trier, 2010).

Beyond disciplines, faculty relationships with students determine their characterization in texts. "The loner" becomes "the enemy" in Inness's (1993, 1994) analysis of women's college novels in the Progressive Era. Inness's work (1993) describes professors in women's college Progressive Era fiction as specifically opposed to and distinct from the student body, they are "outsiders" (p. 114), "disloyal and indifferent" (p. 116) to students' concerns. Without student class alliance or allegiance, faculty are apart from the special community of women, and represented as authority figures who attempt to control women through restrictions and policies that enforce a socially acceptable vision of college femininity (Inness, 1993).

Ranging from bookworm to monster, loner to superstar, many of these faculty types ultimately position professors as "the other" in our popular culture texts, alienated, differentiated, and often "less than" (Reynolds, 2007). Even when professors are portrayed more positively by type, for example, the inspirational teacher or mentor from the student's gaze, deficit is provided through other means. If they are not professionally deficient then deficit is established personally. For example, in *The Mirror Has Two Faces* (1996), Barbra Streisand's character is portrayed as a great teacher. However, the film presents her as a dowdy woman who needs to be physically transformed to attract, or indeed deserve, the attention and affection of a man.

These categories or (stereo)types exploit, engage with, and perpetuate opportunities to (mis)educate consumers of popular culture. The preponderance of more negative faculty types exposes the ambivalence of the professorial image in popular discourse.

Trusting the Professoriate

Professorial (stereo)types in popular culture negotiate notions of trust. Trust and distrust play a powerful part in the depictions of faculty in popular culture providing fertile ground for (mis)education through representation. As part of this, narratives battle with whether professors are good or bad, deliberating the value and role of intellect versus intelligence through various parameters of power imbued by role and institutional hierarchy. The disciplines of professors also provide space to negotiate trust accorded to their role and responsibilities in academia. Portrayals of what professors do, how they do it, where they do it, and why they do it offer many opportunities to (mis)educate.

Good Guys or Bad Guys?

Popular culture presents an ambivalent portrayal of professors by playing with the trustfulness of their depictions through association with the various professorial types and the binary of good and bad. Professorial portrayals present a mixed bag. Weingart, Muhl, and Pansegrau (2003) claim that the good or bad nature of professors depends on the discipline they are associated with in the artifacts of popular culture. Less specifically, Hinton's (1994) work describes professors as collaborators, mentors, and champions for students as well as bullies and narcissistic abusers. While Hinton portrays both good and bad aspects of professorial depiction, Dalton (2007) fails to discern anything good about the cinematic professor claiming that professors are "bad" teachers, portrayed in much the same way as school gym teachers who she describes as "yelling at students, otherwise humiliating students, or engaging in sexual escapades or ridiculous hijinks" (p. 62). Referencing *Real Genius* (1985), *Good Will Hunting* (1998), *Wit* (2001), and *A Beautiful Mind* (2001), Dalton (2007) claims that as "bad" teachers professors distance themselves from their students, exploit others, particularly brilliant students, and remain firmly focused on their self-interests. More focused examinations of the professoriate challenge Dalton's perspective of popular professors who she discusses as part of an in-depth examination of teachers in Hollywood movies focusing mainly on depictions of K–12 teachers (Reynolds, 2007, 2009).

Other work also focuses on the negative. Professors are "snoops" (Conklin, 2009) and "freaks" (Hawlitschka, 2003, p. 98) that cause harm. Professors in *Beverly Hills, 90210* (1990–2000) are uniformly bad to start with or revealed to be so throughout the plot, using students relentlessly (Byers, 2005). Rather than being bad, Tierney (2004) describes professors in academic novels toward the end of the 20th century as weak. Alternatively, Reynolds's (2007) analysis of professors in films 1930–1950 describes a monastic order where professors are dominantly aligned with themes of chastity, calling and sacrifice, and poverty. Harris (2009) continues this theme with her focus on good teachers that includes discussion of vocationally driven "heroic and saintly" (p. 15) depictions of teachers, to which she adds art instructor Katherine in *Mona Lisa Smile* (2003). The distinction between good and bad often relates to professors' (mis)use of their power over students, their work-related choices and motivations (Trier, 2003; Weingart et al., 2003).

Professors' portrayal as good or bad depends on a variety of narrative choices, including the way professors interact with students, their personal choices, as well as their role within the academy. More sophisticated examinations of the trustworthiness of professors move beyond simple examinations of their role as good or bad to consider what contributes to the depiction of them as good or bad, such as the battle between intellect and intelligence.

Intellect Versus Intelligence

A common theme in popular culture research contributing to the perception of trust and the professoriate revolves around the meaning and description of academic aptitude and achievement—what scholars know, how they know it, what they do with it, and how others react to it. Several scholars identify ambivalence facing scholarly pursuits (Reynolds, 2007), distinguishing between being smart and being cool (Franzini, 2008), discussing different types of "smarts" (Radcliff, 2008), ranking academic prowess with practical and technological expertise (Kahlenberg, 2008), and considering knowledge as a gift or commodity (Keroes, 2005). These and other modes of categorizing ways of knowing intimately relates to ideas about trust. Ways of knowing that are perceived as being about intelligence rather than intellect appear more trusted and valued (Radcliff, 2008; Terzian & Grunzke, 2007). Intelligence aligns with a more artistic creativity while intellect is more closely perceived as closely connected to scientific rationality (Terzian & Grunzke, 2007). This division might suggest that professors associated with intelligence gain a trust reprieve in popular culture. Unfortunately, in these cases personal rather than disciplinary shortcomings or dispositions tend to plague professorial depiction. This may provide one explanation for why so many depictions of English professors portray lecherous, damaged individuals despite their association with interpretation and creativity as opposed to science (Carens, 2010; Leuschner, 2006).

Describing the representation of science in biographical and documentary narratives, Radcliff (2008) describes the "polar opposites" he discerns in these narratives that further magnify the intelligence/intellect delineation. I interpret Radcliff's explicit and implicit descriptions as binaries in Table 3. In Radcliff's work, intellect describes the purity and impracticality of scientific research as opposed to the creative and perhaps messy, adaptive genius of intelligence. Distrust for scholarly pursuits in popular culture arises from the manipulation of these binaries, providing ample possibilities for (mis)education.

Radcliff (2008) suggests that only geniuses, such as Einstein, can bridge these binaries successfully in representations. He describes popular culture's rhetoric of exceptionalism that extols Einstein's creativity while simultaneously reinforcing that creativity has no place in "normal" science. The only reason Einstein is able to be both artist and scientist bridging these extremes is through the "hero" narrative of biographies and documentaries.

This rhetoric of exceptionalism is also evident in the media coverage of Madame Curie during her visit to the United States in 1921 (Owens, 2011) and biopics of her life (Elena, 1997). However, the exceptionalist narrative related to Curie in popular culture and media texts, as opposed to Einstein, is that Curie was exceptional not because she balanced art and science but because representations present her balancing science and traditional notions of femininity. Elena (1997) even notes that her traditional and limited portrayal in a 1943 biopic renders the double Nobel Prize–winning Madame Curie as

TABLE 3
Binary Representations of Intellect and Intelligence Based on Radcliff (2008)

Science = Intellect	Art = Intelligence	Binary Descriptions
Usefulness	Creativity	Locus of purpose either intrinsic or extrinsic. Science bears a purpose beyond self whereas the process of creativity retains a purpose in and of itself. Like "learning for learning's sake."
Communal	Individual	Describes the scholarly act where science often involves the many, building on the many, and art does not.
Removed from life	Mindfulness	Scientists isolate themselves from relationships with others and daily concerns versus the mindfulness of art. Mindfulness, being in the moment, embraces sensory experience, engagement with self and others, which may have perhaps been manipulated in more recent popular culture toward more hedonist pursuits.
Deduction	Intuition	Method and logic external to the self define the intellectual process while intelligence derives from within the individual with no defined form or formal process.
Paradigmatically constrained	"Free spirit"	Disciplines and work governed with intelligence not bound by any rules unlike the paradigmatic conventions of science. Paradigmatic change requires a breakthrough by the use of more creative engagement.

"a research assistant who is permanently subordinate to a male scientist" (p. 276).

The different portrayals of intellect and intelligence contribute toward the trust and distrust of popular culture professors. While concentrating on knowledge, manifestations of professorial aptitude ignore the role of depictions of power in contributing to the trust or distrust of professors.

Parameters of Professional Power

Seeking power augurs the downfall of professors in popular culture texts. Whether they seek economic power by the acquisition of wealth, personal power by actively seeking relationships, political power through various machinations, or philosophical power through the single-minded pursuit of knowledge, narratives punish professors who seek to increase their influence (Major, 1998). Professorial power manifests through hierarchical examinations of employment "success" as designated by institutional and position types. These markers of success combine with issues related to tenure as well as the portrayal of research and teaching contributing to the (mis)education of professors through popular culture texts.

The fictional professors work in a profession that has standards and a hierarchy of employment as examined in the third chapter. Professors who work with untraditional students are often portrayed as "losers" or "marginal" academics in mystery novels (Pittman, 1999, p. 84) and popular culture that features community colleges (LaPaglia, 1994; Tucciarone, 2007b). However, continuing ideas about "place" explored in the third chapter and what that might mean, Keroes (2005) in a discussion of *Good Will Hunting* (1997) claims that Robin Williams's character Sean McGuire offers viewers a glimpse of a male community college instructor built around the idea of being a "spiritual leader," a "dissenter," a "man of heart" for whom community college teaching is a "labor of love" (p. 47). So the sense of hierarchy in Keroes's reading of this film becomes a vehicle that embodies positive depictions of community college professors as "men" who care about students, who eschew the elitism of other institutions and their professors to nurture the gifts and possibilities of their students through vocational choice.

Relatedly, professors are also usually portrayed as full-time rather than part-time faculty. LaPaglia (1994) claims that adjunct status is usually another way to indicate a "low-status marker" (p. 96), which is interesting considering that fictional women are often employed in these roles. However, Hynes's *The Lecturer's Tale* (2002) and Kudera's (2011) *Fight for Your Long Day* both use the unstable, roving work of the part-time faculty as the focus for their male protagonist narratives. Hynes's novel particularly highlights and plays on the hierarchical nature of higher education for its narrative choices by giving the lecturer of the title, a man who loses his adjunct job right at the beginning of the novel, the chance to illicitly and secretly bypass hierarchy to get what he wants after an accident to his finger gives it Midas-like powers where his will rather than gold is manifest (Pinsker, 2003).

As the two main areas of professorial work, teaching and research have extreme and ambivalent depictions in popular culture that revolve around training and rank. Regarding training, professors in Hollywood and TV depictions are not always discerned as having different, extended training or expertise in comparison with schoolteachers. Skill and experience as a schoolteacher sometimes renders fluidity between school and university positions so a high school English teacher follows the student character to college in *The Many Loves of Dobie Gillis* (1959–1963) and assumes the role of college English professor (Dalton & Linder, 2008). Scholarship about teachers often conflates the roles of teacher and professor (Bauer, 1998; Dalton, 2007; Harris, 2009; Schwartz, 1960). However, this choice potentially distorts and limits the analysis of this educative role in higher education. Actual schoolteachers and higher education faculty bear different roles, job expectations, and measures for success. It is potentially a fallacy to render higher education professors the same as instead of distinct from schoolteachers. As explored throughout this monograph, just because aspects of popular culture may minimize, misunderstand, and ignore these different roles is all the more reason why scholars should be careful to distinguish between them to provide a more nuanced analysis of the portrayal of teaching for higher education professors as distinct from schoolteachers.

Rather than portrayed as two of the responsibilities of professors, teaching and research are often portrayed in ways that normatively represent research and scholarly pursuits as bad in comparison with teaching as good. Alternatively, scholarship is ignored and teaching retains the distinction of being the professional act of professors. Trier (2003) discusses power in the classroom and its misuse. He analyzes *The Paper Chase* (1973) describing the way the setup of the classroom allows the professor to scrutinize the students, to watch and survey. By controlling where students sit the professor ensures no student can hide. He uses this control to humiliate students, particularly the student protagonist Hart in their first class through interrogation to demonstrate class norms regarding preparedness and participation. The experience is so intense that Hart vomits in the bathroom after class.

Moving beyond the classroom, professors' supervision of students is also a form of teaching that designates power in popular culture texts. Similar to some portrayals of bad teaching, Kelly (2009) illuminates the distant, "master-like" role held by these professors over their graduate students through an analysis of Cham's (1997–) comic strip *Piled Higher and Deeper* as well as novels such as Byatt's *The Biographer's Tale*. Interestingly, though professors are often portrayed as distant from students either in class or through supervisory relationships, narrative arcs sometimes show professors learning from others perhaps more so than they help others learn in films from 1930 until 1958 (Reynolds, 2007; Schwartz, 1960).

As a reward predicated on successful research, teaching, and service, tenure has increasingly provided a hook for hierarchical representations since late 20th century (Tierney, 2004). Tierney (2004) describes the desperation of the professors in these texts to achieve this milestone, an accomplishment authors reinforce by punishing professors with the loss of it when they misbehave, usually thanks to affairs with their students. The novels examined by Tierney (2004) highlight how tenure itself rather than the scholarly products professors create reigns as the raison d'etre for professorial work.

Beyond the ways that institutional roles and responsibilities of professors manifest into a popular culture discourse related to trust due to perceptions of good and bad, ways of knowing, and power, popular culture artifacts also represent demographical possibilities for characteristics or stereotypes that provide opportunities for (mis)education.

White, Straight, and Male: The Professorial Status Quo and Alternative Narratives

Straight, White, male professors overpopulate popular culture higher education. Although European literature includes learned men and male professors before the publishing press was invented (Sheppard, 1990), the acquisition of

TABLE 4
**Numerical Representation of TV Shows Featuring Professors
From 1950 to 2008**

Decade	Number of TV Shows With Male Professors
1950s	3
1960s	6
1970s	12
1980s	10
1990s	19
2000–2008	15

male professorial characters at the beginnings of other media types suggests the enduring relevancy of the profession for popular culture. The first fictional movie using a professor as a character is *The Professor's Fall from Grace* (1899), where the professor as "comic fool" or "buffoon" manifests in the new medium through the presumed contemporaneous hilarity of a farmer's daughter startling a male professor who falls into a barrel of water. From this inglorious beginning in film, the professor remains a popular choice of character in the movies; indeed, between 1930 and 1950 Hollywood produced over 137 films featuring mostly male professors as primary or secondary characters in U.S. movies (Reynolds, 2007). With the gradual proliferation of TV during the 1950s, male professors featured as primary or secondary character roles in at least three shows that decade followed by an increase in subsequent decades (Dalton & Linder, 2008), as represented in Table 4.

In addition to TV and cinematic representation, professors feature as major and secondary characters in a whole host of literature (Kramer, 2000, 2004), being a character that Lyons (1962) describes as "generally a maligned man . . . [who] is usually shown as a timid buffoon guilty of uxoriousness, or a demonic changeling who would employ guile, tyranny, or adultery, to achieve his desires" (p. 132).

TV parallels novels and films by reinforcing the predominantly White male depiction of professors from 1950 to 2008 (Dalton & Linder, 2008) thereby exaggerating and potentially reinforcing a professional imbalance that actually exists (Glazer-Raymo, 2001, 2008). Although women faculty and faculty of color gradually move from nonexistent to a limited, restrained but increased presence throughout the 20th century to date, Tobolowsky's (2012) analysis of TV episodes from 10 series airing from 1998 to 2010 emphasizes the overrepresentation of White males in general, not only within the medium but also startlingly in comparison with actual professorial demographics. Therefore, TV amplifies the presence of male professors in ways that (mis)educate regarding their participation in the profession.

The disciplines of TV male professors appear fairly diverse and they monopolize broad and deep portrayals across fields. Table 5 represents the range of depictions based on Dalton and Linder's (2008) description of teachers on TV. I generated this table by cross-referencing all the titles of the TV shows with descriptions of them to identify professors, distinct from schoolteachers, if the Dalton and Linder text did not disclose the institutional placement of these TV teachers.

Tension exists between teaching and research in depictions of professors and subsequent scholarly literature. Professors in Hollywood and TV depictions, as well as some scholarly writings, are not shown having any more extended training or expertise than schoolteachers.

The representation of male faculty in popular culture collectively represents all aspects of professorial work. In the movies, male professors teach (e.g., *The Male Animal*, 1942; *The Paper Chase*, 1973; *Wonder Boys*, 2000), research (e.g., *The Nutty Professor*, 1963 and 1996; *The Body Disappears*, 1941; *Good Will Hunting*, 1997; *Kinsey*, 2004; *A Beautiful Mind*, 2001), and write books (e.g., *The Feminine Touch*, 1941; *Apartment for Peggy*, 1948; *The Mirror Has Two Faces*, 1996; *Wonder Boys*, 2000). Although male professorial representation shows them engaged in a range of faculty responsibilities, some work emphasizes their role as teacher, perhaps related to the students' gaze discussed in the third chapter (Carens, 2010; Dalton, 2007). Others emphasize male professors' complete disinterest in teaching focusing on scholarly products through their research and writing, with male professors often portrayed as bad teachers (or people) but successful scholars (Dagaz & Harger, 2011; Tierney, 2004).

Research suggests that a continuum may exist for the portrayal of male professors. Work focusing on film from 1930 to 1950 aligns male professors

TABLE 5
Professors' TV Disciplines Adapted From Dalton and Linder (2008)

Discipline		TV Shows
STEM		*3rd Rock from the Sun* (1996–2001)
		Felicity (1998–2002)
		Heroes (2006–2010)
		Nanny and the Professor (1970–1971)
		Numb3rs (2005–2010)
		Two of a Kind (1998–1999)
English		*Doctor, Doctor* (1989–1991)
		Meet Mr. McNutley (1953–1955)
		Mr. Sunshine (1986)
		October Road (2007–2008)
		Please don't eat the daisies (1965–1967)
		The Preston Episodes (1995)
		Two (1996–1997)
Anthropology		*Gideon Oliver* (1989)
		Saved by the Bell: the College Years (1993–1994)
		The Jimmy Stewart Show (1971–1972)
History		*Brother's Keeper* (1998–1999)
		The Education of Max Bickford (2001–2002)
		Pursuit of Happiness (1987–1988)
Other	Agriculture	*Roots: The Next Generation* (1979)
	Classics	*thirtysomething* (1987–1991)
	Communications	*The Parent'Hood* (1995–1998)
	Criminology	*Snoops* (1989–1990)
	Drama	*The Ray Milland Show* (1953–1955)
	Law	*The Paper Chase* (1978–1986)
	Parapsychology	*Ghost Whisperer* (2005–2010)
		Sixth Sense (1972)
	Psychology	*That's Life* (2000–2002)
	Sexuality	*The Bedford Diaries* (2006)

with a monastic "order of the professoriate" where the dominant themes allied with the professors cast them as safe others in need of transformation (Reynolds, 2007). However, Dagaz and Harger's (2011) focus on the cinematic 1985–2005 finds that film narratives from this period depict male professors "ranging from hegemonic masculinity to bookish nerd" (p. 281). Perhaps like the safe/scary representations of institutions, a similar visual serves

FIGURE 4
Male Professor Representation Throughout the 20th Century to 2005

Early 20th century:	**PRIESTLY**	←→	hegemonic masculinity
Later in the 20th century:	priestly	**←→**	**HEGEMONIC MASCULINITY**

to depict the collective representation of male professors in the movies (see Figure 4).

Reinforcing this possible dominant and alternative continuum, Tierney (2004) describes professors in academic novels of the late 20th century as "sexually ravenous men who may be productive scholars, but are seriously flawed human beings" (p. 174). The professors in the novels he examines find students and teaching "irrelevant" (p. 172) remaining focused on the goal of tenure.

Alternative Male Narratives

Popular culture portrays a gradual but limited awareness that the professorial role extends beyond heterosexual White males. Male faculty of color have started to gain a wider foothold in popular culture as typified by George Takei's turn as an economics professor in *Larry Crowne* (2011) or Sendhil Ramamurthy's geneticist in TV's *Heroes* (2006–2010) but these portrayals are rare with Dagaz and Harger (2011) claiming that only two Asian professors and one Hispanic professor appear in films between 1985 and 2005.

African Americans dominate the portrayal of male professors of color; indeed despite locating only 12 African American professors in eight films from a sample of 89 U.S. films from 1985 to 2005, Dagaz and Harger (2011) claim that African American professors are overrepresented in film in comparison with their actual presence in higher education. Possibly the first portrayal of an African American professor occurred in Hollywood in the all-Black cast *Beware* (1946). In this film one Black male professor teaches several disciplines more akin to an elementary school teacher than a specialized professor (Reynolds, 2007). However, though some artifacts explore race on campus such as *Higher Learning* (1995), most scholarship focusing on popular culture and higher education to date does not distinguish the race of characters within the cultural texts. Identifying racial differences indicates the gradual challenge to the status quo while simultaneously recognizing its continued strength, despite changes in society and academia. In TV, possibly the first African American professorial character is a male agricultural professor working at an HBCU in *Roots: The Next Generation* (1979–1981) (Dalton & Linder, 2008). This first TV portrayal 30 years after *Beware* is suggestive of inclusion but limits through the alignment of discipline and institutional placement as this first Black TV professor appears in a field of practical use (agriculture) in segregated academic space (an HBCU). The 1980s continues to be more inclusive of the intersections of race and role in higher education depicting at least three shows with African American professors out of the 10 higher education related shows started in the decade (see Table 4). Discipline and placement progress in the 1980s portrays African American professors at a variety of institutions and expanded disciplines including various professors from different disciplines at an HBCU in *A Different World* (1987–1993), an anthropologist working at Columbia University (*Gideon Oliver*, 1989–1989), and a criminologist at a university in Washington, DC, in *Snoops* (1989–1990) (Dalton & Linder, 2008).

After James Earl Jones's professorial turn in *Soul Man* (1986), the portrayal of Black male professors also increased in cinematic representation from the 1990s in movies ranging from physical comedy and science fiction to hard-hitting dramas, all set in different institutional types. Table 6 highlights these movies and interestingly emphasizes the repeat performances of two African American actors, as well as a surprising inclusion in this list. In *The Human Stain* (2003), Anthony Hopkins plays a light-skinned African American professor who "passes" as White throughout his academic career. Considering the minimal representation of Black men as professors in the movies, it is ironic that one of those few portrayals casts a White Welshman.

The slow and gradual inclusion of depictions of professorial sexuality beyond a heteronormative lens reflects the awareness and increasing acceptance of queer identities in the United States throughout the period of study for this monograph. In TV, sexuality is avoided in early programming and narratives are predicated on heteronormativity. Male professors were married to

TABLE 6
Black Professors in the Movies at the End of the 20th Century and Early 21st Century

Release Date	Film Title	Actor
1995	*Higher Learning*	Lawrence Fishburne
1996	*The Nutty Professor*	Eddie Murphy
2000	*The Nutty Professor II: The Klumps*	Eddie Murphy
2001	*Evolution*	Orlando Jones
2002	*Drumline*	Orlando Jones
2003	*The Human Stain*	Anthony Hopkins
2007	*The Man from Earth*	Tony Todd
2007	*The Great Debaters*	Denzel Washington

women or widowed in the earliest shows (Dalton & Linder, 2008). Unlike films of the 1930s and 1940s where narratives transform younger male professors from chaste "othered" priest figures to desirable heterosexual love interests (Reynolds, 2007), TV portrays male professors already transformed and established as a "man" as inferred through their success in the marriage market. This heterosexist lens is only challenged in the 1980s where perhaps the first openly gay TV professor is found in the show "Doctor, Doctor" (1989–1991) as the English professor brother of one of the main characters (Dalton & Linder, 2008). This is a strategy repeated in *The Good Wife* (2009–), where the "wife's" gay brother is also a professor. Often pushing the edge of wider-audience understanding, *The Education of Max Bickford* (2001–2002) introduced a transgendered professorial character as the best friend of the title character (Dalton & Linder, 2008). Interestingly, several 21st-century depictions provide an interesting counterpoint to earlier depictions of professors as priestly through post-sexual characterizations of the professor as widowed professors who need transformation, usually through new love or meaningful reengagement with others (e.g., *Fishtales*, 2008; *Smart People*, 2008; *The Visitor*, 2007).

Although homoerotic narratives have featured young men in college from at least earlier in the 20th century (e.g., *Brideshead Revisited*, 1945), TV and film depictions of gay professors are scant in mainstream productions, while scholarly discussion of the portrayal of gay professors examining the intersection of sexuality with academic role in popular culture appears to be nonexistent. *Little Miss Sunshine* (2006) follows TV's "gay brother" trend with Steve Carrell's depiction of a suicidal Proust scholar. More recently, the film *A Single Man* (2009) provides a rare mainstream focus on a gay professor, featuring Colin Firth's Oscar-nominated performance. An adaption of Isherwood's 1964 novel, *A Single Man* provides a frank look at homosexuality, longing, loss, and love from the perspective of a grieving professor.

Heteronormativity governs the portrayal of male academics in popular culture, particularly in films and TV, but the late 20th century sees a tiny, peripheral infiltration in representation. Race and sexuality provide some alternate representations to the metadepiction of professors but the presence of women faculty provides the most visible challenge.

The Pop Culture Ceiling: Gendered Challenges to the Status Quo

Although popular culture's female professors bear many of the characteristics of professors in general, they also contend with differences in representation, similar to the way actual female professors experience gendered differences in their academic lives (Glazer-Raymo, 2001, 2008). Popular culture presents a minimized presence with limited options for women faculty related to where they work and what they do.

Women's early and continued portrayal as faculty is scant. Women first appear as faculty in literature at the turn of the 20th century and move into cinematic portrayals as early as 1932 with several strong movie portrayals during the 1940s (Inness, 1995; Marchalonis, 1995; Reynolds, 2009). Indeed, female faculty representation as the major protagonist is far more diverse than male faculty representation in some ways during the 1930s and 1940s offering portrayals of a junior college in *That Hagen Girl* (1947), a woman's college in *Bathing Beauty* (1944), and state institutions in *The Age of Consent* (1932), *The Accused* (1948), and *Yes Sir, That's my Baby* (1949) (Reynolds, 2007, 2009). In TV, Dalton and Linder (2008) claim that Ray Milland's professorial character interacts with "female colleagues" in his 1950s show but the authors' first description of a female professor is a sociology professor in *The Many Loves of Dobie Gillis* (1959–1963). Initially, in these roles, female faculty take care of female students, live with them in dormitories, and several are presented as hiding in higher education away from the attentions of men, so their cloistered job becomes both sanctuary and sacrifice (Reynolds, 2009).

Female professors increase in visibility throughout the late 20th and early 21st centuries through mystery novels where they are the major protagonist (e.g., Amanda Cross novels) and visual portrayals where celebrated actresses play female academics such as Barbra Streisand in *The Mirror Has Two Faces* (1996), Julia Roberts in *Mona Lisa Smile* (2003) and *Larry Crowne* (2011), and Emma Thompson in *Wit* (2001). Marchino (1989) suggests that the academic mystery novel with female professor detectives represents a critique of the patriarchal academy where the murder, mayhem, and retribution narratively imagined, often by actual female professor authors, serve to demonstrate "a basic critique of male misuse of power and a focusing of attention on the representative of patriarchal oppression" (p. 94). Alternatively, visual portrayals do not challenge male professorial dominance. Although the TV show *Undeclared* (2001–2003) portrayed several different faculty members, none are women. Individual movies or TV shows with female leads do occur but more often women faculty may be shown sitting at the table with their male counterparts with minimal or silent roles in the narrative (Tobolowsky, 2012).

Interestingly, but not surprisingly, the most powerful depictions of female faculty are written by female faculty themselves. A recent example includes Deborah Harkness's bestselling fantasy *All Souls Trilogy* started in 2011. Harkness is a renowned historian who has tapped into the popularity of magic, witches, and vampires epitomized by the success of the *Harry Potter* and *Twilight* series by writing books for adults with these characters. The major characters are both professors, focusing on a Yale historian who is a powerful female witch and an Oxford scientist who is a 1500-year-old male vampire. Perhaps popular novels like Harkness's *All Souls Trilogy* pave the way forward for popular culture female academics with the portrayal of smart female academics whose scholarship, prowess, and academic power are emphasized without deferring to traditional notions of femininity and related roles.

The institutional placement of popular culture's female faculty locates women at a variety of institutional types but women's colleges and community colleges particularly offer a home to female fictional academics as protagonist (Inness, 1995; LaPaglia, 1994; Marchalonis, 1995). Although mostly bit parts, female faculty alternatively support and restrain students in college novels of the early 20th century, often championing the status quo for college women's options and aptitudes (Marchalonis, 1995). These female faculty control and limit their charges.

Tobolowsky (2012) points out that women faculty and faculty of color are actually overrepresented in TV primetime community college depiction in comparison with their actual employment, although men are still the majority of the portrayals. This is consistent with recent movies where stories set around community colleges feature female professors. Julia Roberts and Uma Thurman both star as community college professors in *Larry Crowne* (2011) and *The Life Before Her Eyes* (2007), respectively. In fact, of the three main professors the audience sees at the community college in *Larry Crowne*, two are women. In community college fiction up until 1992, LaPaglia (1994) claims that White men who specialize in English are the majority of professors but her description of "good faculty" in community college narratives comprises examples of stories featuring women and an African American male faculty member. These descriptions suggest that any sense of vocation and accomplishment for women and minority scholars is dependent on institutional type and these academics working in culturally defined lower hierarchical "place," as discussed in the third chapter.

Female academics are almost exclusively represented as teachers. Scholarship, writing, and research play a limited role in female professorial representation. Rose Morgan, Barbra Streisand's character in *The Mirror Has Two Faces* (1996), demonstrates her professorial credentials through her charismatic and inspirational lecture and interaction with students in a scene where she captivates a packed auditorium. Her male counterpart in the movie demonstrates his academic credentials through his book preview and demonstration of mathematical expertise but his teaching is dismal, not engaging students. While his teaching improves thanks to her mentorship and advice, the viewer does not see or hear of her research, or the books and scholarship that she contributes alongside her teaching to be able to maintain her position. Unlike her male colleague, Rose's work is limited to that of teacher, to both students and other faculty, a role Bauer (1998) describes as sexualized pedagogy. When women are presented as more scholarly they are narratively punished such as in *Wit* (2001) or *Little Man Tate* (2007) by an attack on their femininity, on their ability to care, and their emotive capacities (Dalton, 2007). Relatedly, Dagaz and Harger (2011) offer three main stereotypical depictions of female professors in films from 1985 to 2005 as masculinized, sexualized, or feminized roles. In feminized roles women are caretakers and display emotion, while the masculinized roles depict the professors as "no-nonsense" characters who have power over students' progress. The authors relate these characteristics to disciplinary differences where literature professors are sexualized, humanities professors are feminized, and women in male-dominated professions are masculinized (p. 282).

The appearance of female faculty contributes to the maintenance of the stereotypes related to female professors. Research focusing on earlier depictions of female professors might include "the old maid" as a stereotypical portrayal. However, these portrayals were not necessarily focused on age but on appearance where style, clothing, and priorities require transformations (Flicker, 2003; Reynolds, 2009). Appearance also indicates the feminized, sexualized, and masculinized portrayal of female professors (Dagaz & Harger, 2011). Steinke (2005) describes the sexualization of female scientists, many of whom are professors, through appearance. She outlines how most of the characters in her sample are attractive female scientists or the film narrative provides a scene of transformation to allow the male protagonist to see past their brains. The bodies of female professors, attractive or not, are sources for narratives to demonstrate disapproval with their chosen profession, with their disregard of traditional gendered roles. In the 1940s, this was demonstrated by the attempted rape of a professor in *The Accused* (1948) and in the 2000s through illness, specifically ovarian cancer where the professor in *Wit*, both the play and subsequent film, is humiliated by a former student giving her a pelvic exam (Leuschner, 2006; Reynolds, 2009).

Narratives find different ways of portraying women as lesser professorial figures. As well as limiting women to the role of teacher, the broader skills of female professors are also minimized in a variety of ways. Some faculty at women's colleges in fiction of the 1920s and 1930s are underwhelming in their abilities and their expectations for students. In Millay's novel *Against the Wall* (1929) faculty actively restrain a student's intellectual curiosity to the point where she leaves for another institution (Marchalonis, 1995). Female scientists are often portrayed as helpers for male scientists in labs rather than the lead researcher on projects (Flicker, 2003). Steinke (2005) described a more equal role for women scientists in her sample of films but noticed that research teams and labs only ever have one female representative in the team, with multiple men, so women are less through being an exception to a masculinized rule.

Literature focusing on artifacts that feature female professors also minimizes the gendered barriers that limited narratives depict in popular culture. In *The Songcatcher* (2001) the major protagonist, a female musicologist working at an urban institution, bashes against the glass ceiling of her department and retreats to her sister's rural school where she discovers a vibrant, living trove of undiscovered Appalachian songs. This 2001 Sundance Film Festival winner presents the professor as "liberal-liberator" where she appropriates and commodifies the songs of an Appalachian community in a colonial-esque ignorance of privilege (Britt & Tunagur, 2011). Although described as "oppressed" in her urban university life in Britt and Tunagur's (2011) analysis of *The Songcatcher*, the authors claim, "the film (and by extension its maker) seems to mistake its protagonist as belonging to the sphere of the disenfranchised" (p. 166). The authors deny the salience of gender and professorial experience within the academic sphere as presented in this film.

Other portrayals destabilize the abilities of female faculty by depicting challenges to their authority and knowledge (Reynolds, 2009; Ryan & Townsend, 2010). Male students in *The Accused* (1948) and *Teacher's Pet* (1958) both confront their female faculty members and, as mentioned previously, the student in *The Accused* goes so far as to attempt to rape his professor. In addition to challenge and violent attacks, romance is another way narratives destabilize women professors' authority and expertise. Many popular culture narratives feature female professors seeking, acquiring, or engaging in relationships. In fact, Steinke (2005) found that the narratives involving women scientists overwhelmingly featured romance with 20 out of 23 films generating these storylines.

Female professors in TV representations remain in feminized disciplines and roles. For example, Felicity's only female professor is her art professor (*Felicity*, 1998–2001), the only female professor in *The Bedford Diaries* (2006–2006) is an African American woman chairing the ethics committee, in *3rd Rock from the Sun* (1996–2001) John Lithgow's officemate turned dean is an anthropology professor, a female professor of English appears in *Kelly Kelly* (1998), and *The Many Loves of Dobbie Gillis* (1959–1963) provides a sociology professor (Dalton & Linder, 2008). In these TV examples female faculty expertise allies with feminized disciplines, those that do not stray too far away from traditional notions of women's sphere demonstrated through expertise about the human condition and the arts, their oft-aligned role as moral arbitrator, and in disciplines that are disparaged in popular culture. A more recent stereotype evolves the feminized professor to one of "the feminist" professor presenting female professors as extreme, male-disparaging, and women-centered teachers (e.g., *Greek*, 2007–2011; *Sorority Boys*, 2002).

Media imagery related to actual professors battles ideas of femininity and discipline particularly in the descriptions of and fascination about Madame Curie. Biographers of Curie claim that she was solely represented as a typical woman in U.S. coverage of her trip to the United States in 1921 with a focus on family responsibilities and her role of wife, but Owens (2011) argues that his analysis of 267 news articles from a variety of newspapers and magazines regarding coverage of Madame Curie's trip challenges her biographers' approaches. Owens (2011) claims, "the daily press told them [readers] of a motherly, saint-like figure, while *Scientific Monthly* told them of a powerful, female scientist" (p. 117). Medium and audience influence the message of narratives about female academics.

Women professors also act as moral arbitrators in their representations. Bosco (2007) describes how a female academic acts as angel, confessor, and facilitator in L'Heureux's *The Handmaid of Desire* where descriptions of her nun-like appearance, use of religious language, and symbolism cast her as aiding in the reconstruction of vocation for the other professors in this novel. Additionally, in mystery novels women professors in the role of female academic "sleuths" challenge and reinforce traditional roles for women both within the academy and socially. Marchino (1989) describes these women as collectively "excellent teachers" but they also use their scholarly expertise and research acumen to solve crimes on campus. Gender climate particularly at the time of publication of Marchino's article displays a battle for equitable recognition through pay, publication, and tenure that often positions male faculty as the perpetrators in these novels. Interestingly, as well as moral arbitration, faculty detectives demonstrate a practical use for research skills and scholarly expertise that nonacademics relate to. Female academic sleuths champion women's role within the academy with authors playing with the figurative idea of professors as detectives in their literal depiction of them as such (Maier, 1999; Marchino, 1989). Perhaps detective novels, particularly those written by academics, provide a way for nonacademics to understand the role, function, and specialties of professors.

The exploration of women's role and values as professors in popular culture situate female faculty in contradictory and pointed ways, as saintly and sexual, motherly and masculine, as well as incompetent and ideal. Possibilities for (mis)education abound as these women teach rather than research and if they stray from this sphere of responsibility they can be narratively punished through alignment with masculine traits or lonely, narrow lives where their profession is their only sphere of limited influence and experience.

Challenging the White, Straight Female Status Quo: Alternative Narratives

Even more so than with men, alternate depictions of female faculty beyond a heteronormative White privileged text are limited. The "invisibility" of lesbian faculty in popular culture in general uniquely resonates with ideas about place and higher education. Young (2005) analyzes two films with female professors who embrace a lesbian relationship and identity, forgoing their heterosexual identity and relationships during the films. As films that trace sexual awakening and self-knowledge, the narratives intersect characteristics of academia with heteronormativity so that the professors' fear, conservatism, rigidity, control, sterility, and orderliness reflect that of academia and their suppression of a lesbian identity. An interesting allusion subverts the "sacred space" idea described in the third chapter to one where the women take that separate space with them in the way that they live their lives so the women hide themselves away with their books, and use them as a barrier to others and their own awareness of their burgeoning sexual identity. Clothing and manner reinforce this intersection with the women's growing embrace of a lesbian identity reflected in physical changes with clothing and hair styles as well as behavior choices common in professorial narrative transformations, for example, moving from inaction to action. In contrast, the syndicated comic *Dykes to Watch Out For* (1987–2008) features lesbian professors completely comfortable with their sexuality, out to students, and actively engaged in the gay community (http://dykestowatchoutfor.com/dtwof).

Representations of female faculty of color remain rare and marginal. Perhaps the first visual depiction of a female instructor of color in higher education occurs in *Beware* (1946). This all-Black cast film set in an HBCU depicts a light-skinned, young woman as a physical education instructor who is rescued by romance from this position during the narrative (Reynolds, 2009). Forty years later *A Different World* (1987–1993) depicts an African American woman as a chemistry professor before Eddie Murphy's *Nutty Professor II: The Klumps* (2000) features Janet Jackson as his colleague and girlfriend. Echoing the absence of real and persistent images of women of color in film and TV, there is an absence of academic writing about these limited depictions. Tobolowsky (2012) notes the minimization of female faculty but particularly female faculty of color in the TV shows she examined.

A popular culture champion for faculty of color can be found in the novels of Pamela Thomas-Graham. She writes mystery novels about a sleuthing African American female economics professor at Harvard, the first of which is *A Darker Shade of Crimson* (1998). *Relic Hunter* (1999–2002) also provides a notable exception to the minimization of female faculty of color that has received scholarly attention. In this TV show Tia Carrere plays Sydney Fox, a "Eurasian female hero(ine)" of a history professor who studies ancient civilizations (Jiwani, 2005). As well as teaching in the classroom she also whizzes about the globe retrieving "relics" and using her black belt martial arts prowess to fight off the bad guys (Jiwani, 2005). Jiwani (2005) describes the success of this show and the power of featuring a woman of color as the swashbuckling protagonist. This show uses the position of the professor to fight against as well as appropriate colonialism. Sydney Fox as a Eurasian lead demolishes the fetish of the exoticized other while embodying the colonial tendency to appropriate goods from differently educated others under the guise of aid or protection (Jiwani, 2005).

Representations of women faculty challenge the male dominance of professorial ranks in higher education but still face hurdles for wider, equally skilled representation in popular culture, particularly those faculty who differ from a White, straight majority. Popular culture's imbalance in representation bears numerous messages about inclusion and exclusion for female faculty that contribute to (mis)education.

Concluding Thoughts

Popular culture's professors provide ample opportunities for (mis)education exhibiting explicit and implicit messages about who a professor is and what they do. These messages influence viewer/consumer expectations about behavior, expertise, skills, and aptitudes related to role, gender, race, and sexuality that include and exclude. Portrayals (mis)educate concerning the trustworthiness of professors and their intellectual pursuits contending with whether professors are good or bad and whether they can be trusted, through representations that range from priestly to literally monstrous in characterization. The depictions regarding the work of professors is potentially the most damaging for possibilities of (mis)education where cultural texts contest the value and worth of professorial work and limit professorial roles. Teaching is often displayed as the sole occupation of faculty and depictions of research engagement align with teaching disengagement or questionable ethics. Worryingly, White, heterosexual male overrepresentation exaggerates the invisibility of women and minorities in the academy portraying higher education as less diverse than it is, which challenges its ability to be inclusive and provides questions about who belongs that are also echoed in the portrayal of college students in popular culture.

Learning From "U": College Students in Popular Culture

Introduction

F ROM PICTURES OF 19TH century collegiate athletes on the covers of *Harper's Weekly* in the 1850s (Messenger, 1981) to college football films of the late 1920s–1940 (Miller, 2010), and 21st-century films and TV shows (Conklin, 2008), much of the popular culture texts featuring higher education in some way, and the literature about them, implicitly or explicitly portrays that a college student is male, White, and heterosexual, just like the major portrayal of professors. College students are usually traditionally aged students, young people heading to higher education straight after high school. Throughout the 20th century, students not embodying these characteristics move from complete invisibility to visibility in specialized arenas (e.g., college women's novels and African American magazines) or provide peripheral, token, and increasingly wider and more central representation. However, scholarly discussions often reinforce the White, straight, young, male collegian instead of challenging it as evidenced by Lyons's (1962) and Messenger's (1981) dismissal of college women's novels, a position decried by other scholars (Inness, 1993; Marchalonis, 1995). Umphlett's (1984) examination of college movies also provides an exemplar of this observation as the sleeve pictures chosen to adorn, represent, and market his book about college life in the movies contain only White men.

This chapter explores the college student in popular culture discussing identity and status as defining characteristics of fictional students, and the related themes of privilege and gender performance attributed to their portrayals. In many ways the student portrayals align with the depictions of institutional types discussed in the third chapter, as characteristics and themes work with the ideas of separation and inclusion, alienation and belonging, and young people's next stages in life after high school. As the portrayal of institutions often relies on a student gaze to focus the narrative and define higher education, so too does the student gaze provide a certain perspective for position-taking regarding a selfish or selfless higher education that frames students' college experience in popular culture.

Possibilities for (mis)education abound as college student representation in popular culture frames and reframes through time and media who belongs in higher education and what they do (or do not do) there.

Shaping Popular Culture College Students Through Institutional Status

Organizational structures of institutions of higher education provide one way of characterizing college students in popular culture, endowing them with characteristics aligned with specific institutions as well as distinct organizing features of college life that indicate place, role, and potentially ongoing value.

Being an Undergraduate Student

A popular culture college student is overwhelmingly undergraduate enjoying a "golden life" (Lyons, 1962, p. 23) in college novels pre-1962, a trend that continues in 21st-century TV where none of the characters in *Greek* (2007–2011) consistently have part-time jobs or worry about money. The only time extended focus on money is given in *Greek's* narrative is when one of the privileged wealthy students gives up his trust fund to be able to make his own choices. This focus mirrors the attention given to former rich students who have fallen on bad times in late 19th- and early 20th-century novels (Inness, 1995).

The (stereo)types written about concerning college students tend to delineate between academic mission, student activities and abilities, and the tension between an institutions' academic mission and students' projected participation, as discussed in social and academic tension of the third chapter. As illustrated in Table 7, these terms all have something to do with one of three student dynamics: academics, social life, or college activities. In addition to those in the table, types of women students also align with popular cultural shorthand that are not limited to the portrayal of college students regarding appearance and (heteronormative) desirability such as "the fat/plain friend," "the beauty," and "the ugly duckling/swan."

The types described in Table 7 are not exhaustive but they do identify common types of undergraduate students portrayed in popular culture from the mid-1800s to the early 21st century and written about in scholarly research. Most of these types should be familiar from experience with artifacts of popular culture. Rather than being included in the umbrella "affiliated" label, "The Activist" stands alone due to the attention paid to this subgroup of student characters in literature about higher education (Conklin, 2008; Umphlett, 1984) where these students play important roles in popular culture especially in periods of intense actual protest. Veteran students in popular culture provide one example of "Affiliated" students that receive group attention in cultural artifacts, particularly in the 1940s and 1950s. Most movies and novels portray this group of adult students with respect despite their difference in age from the traditional students, representing veterans as exhibiting a seriousness of purpose and desire to do well in school that is a strength rather than a deficit (Pittman & Osborn, 2000).

Illustrated by veteran students, the portrayal of students and the salience of different types varies according to the time of its making, reflecting an ensuing shifting cultural relevancy, hinting at changing representations in different periods. For example, Hinton (1994) argues that the portrayal of students from 1960 to 1990 moves in the early 1960s from a social, communal, group portrayal to alienation and angst later in the decade before films representing student rebellion in 1970. Then, the rest of the 1970s focuses on a nostalgic portrayal of students before the materialistic portrayal of the 1980s. The 1980s also shows different groups of students that, instead of assimilating as in the early 1960s films from outsider to insider, form their own groups, particularly emphasized by the liberated "nerd" portrayals.

TABLE 7
Typology of Students in Popular Culture

The Relationship	Student Type	Description
College students and academic focus/prowess	The Fusser, Grinder, Bore, or Planner	Students who work hard and appreciate the academic opportunity provided by college.
	The Shark, Wiz-kid, Brainiac or Smarts	The smart students. Some work hard to excel, others find college material easy. Some help other students by choice or find themselves leveraged into helping arrangements by the promise of something desired.
	The Nerd or Geek	Can also be smart but not necessarily. Nerd or geek can also indicate a focus on technology, science fiction, or single-minded interaction with perceived fringe interests.
	The Stupid, Dumb, Idiot or Mouth Breathers	Students portrayed as lacking the comprehension skills and aptitude for the simplest situations let alone college academic work.
	The Undecided, Lost, Directionless, or Pathless	Typified by the question "what am I going to do with my life?," this type manifests in college texts through major choice indecision and change as well as angst about the future and how their present contributes to it.
College students and social focus	The Slacker	Skates by, lazes around, misses class, doesn't really participate in college life.
	The Partyer	For this student, actively engaging in a good time is paramount. Therefore, in popular culture college is purely about the opportunity for, often hedonistic, excess.
	The Rake, Sure Thing, Virgin Whisperer, Slut, Girl/Boy Friend, Friend with Benefits, One Night Stand, etc.	Intimate encounters and exploration are the focus of these students either as conquests or as part of meaningful partnerships.

(Continued)

TABLE 7
Continued

The Relationship	Student Type	Description
College students with activities and participation	The Athlete Hero, Brute, or Jock	Participation in sports defines these students' college experience. Usually a male student who excels on the field either as the hero or the crusher. Early fiction delineated between hero and brute, more recent narratives collapse the type to one of "jock."
	The Greek	Participation in Greek life defines these students' college experiences.
	The All-round Girl, Gibson Girl, or Athletic Girl	Athletic, popular women.
	The Bluestocking, Activist or Community Volunteer	Students with a cause that prompts them to action, peaceful or violent. Perhaps naïvely or unsophisticatedly, think about others and act accordingly.
	The Affiliated or "fill in the blank" participant	Rather than a specific type, these students identified by membership to a group not related to college or promote whatever college activity or group they are part of in the narrative, akin to Greek life but without the singular body of artifacts, e.g., student paper, student government, and student job.

These types illustrate how some characteristics bear possibilities for (mis)education about undergraduate students. They present templates of characters indicating worth and value in the academic community that could influence choices and behaviors.

Being Graduate Students

Types for graduate students of popular culture align with the Wiz-kid and/or Nerd categories of undergraduates. However, characteristics of graduate students notably reflect, minimize, and exaggerate their actual roles and purpose within higher education. Graduate students work on research, write, read, and teach in TV, film, comics, and novels but more extended descriptions or analyses of college life ignore or minimize their role in popular culture's higher education (Conklin, 2008).

Popular culture often portrays graduate students as slaves to the whims, needs, and use of their professors at elite institutions (Keroes, 2005). Interestingly, this is something explored in the film *The Addiction* (1995) where a PhD student becomes a vampire during her program and feeds upon her committee at her dissertation defense. Through the protagonist's vampiric change the film explores the transforming and addictive power of knowledge while questioning the utility of academia (Daspit & Weaver, 2005; McDermott & Daspit, 2005). Byers (1996) notes the increase of female graduate students in TV in the 1990s and describes these characters as grotesque, relational, and hysterical in their representation, all of which contribute to their depiction as outsiders or imposters in the academy.

The comic *Piled Higher and Deeper* (Cham, 1997–) illustrates relationships between graduate students and professors. Cham's comics portray graduate students as anonymous, tongue-tied supplicants who labor over nonacademic menial work to get their advisor's approval while simultaneously collapsing under the pressure of graduate work indicated through chronic procrastination (Kelly, 2009). Perhaps, similarly to professors, discipline affects the portrayal of graduate students, as unlike Cham's science field graduate students, Bosco (2007) describes those from the humanities in academic novels as affected, earnest, and superior rejecting course offerings not considered exotic enough for their developed tastes.

Limited research explores graduate students in popular culture and although undergraduates may have inspired a greater quantity of cultural texts and research about them does not mean that graduate students lack representation. In addition to the comic and film mentioned already, TV, movies, and novels portray graduate students in numerous and diverse narratives as demonstrated in Table 8.

Exceptions to the separation of undergraduates and graduates usually revolve around romance or sex where graduate students TAing for classes inevitably engage in relationships or sex with undergraduate students in the class (e.g., *Answer This!*, 2011), although graduate students seem to prefer

TABLE 8
Examples of Graduate Students in Popular Culture

Media	Artifact Examples
TV	*Beverly Hills 90210* (1990–2000)
	Bones (from 2005)
	Cheers (1982–1983)
	Greek (2007–2011)
	Numb3rs (2005–2010)
	Party of 5 (1994–2000)
	Siberia (2013)
	The Big Bang Theory (2007)
	The Paper Chase (1978–1986)
Movies	*Answer This!* (2011)
	Flatliners (1990)
	Jurassic Park III (2001)
	Legally Blonde (2001)
	Losing Control (2011)
	Marathon Man (1976)
	Nancy, Please (2011)
	Patch Adams (1998)
	PhD (Piled Higher and Deeper) (2013)
	Proof (2005)
	Starting out in the Evening (2007)
	The Oxford Murders (2008)
	The Paper Chase (1973)
Novels	Baron's *Lilly Sampson Mystery Series* (starting in 2002)
	Choi's *My Education* (2013)
	Kingsolver's *Flight Behavior* (2012)
	Willig's *Pink Carnation* series (starting in 2005 and at 10 books in 2013)

relationships with their professors or other graduate students for their part-ners or conquests in movies (e.g., *The Pelican Brief,* 1993; *The Nutty Professor,* 1996; *Elegy,* 2008).

ABC Family's *Greek* (2007–2011) plays with the differentiation between undergraduate and graduate students with two of the main characters having ill-fated relationships with graduate students. The portrayal of graduate students in this show juxtaposes their increased maturity and security regarding their identities, desires, and choices with the undergraduates' comparable im-maturity. Naturally, for a show focused on undergraduate life this difference translates the graduate students as too serious, too pushy, or too scary from the undergraduate protagonists' perspective.

Being Special

Although popular culture increasingly diffuses the salience of university and class-year identity throughout texts of the 20th century, the continued valorization of Ivy League schools maintains a hold on the meaning-making and embedded identity claims of the fictional students who attend them. Identifying a student as one who attends Harvard or other institutions meant something in 1900 (Anderson & Clark, 2012) and it still means something in popular culture texts of the 2000s. Naturally, meanings change during this period. Student identification with a specific institution early in the 20th century related to distinct characteristics, so being a Yale man meant something specific and was differentiated from being a man of Princeton. In the late 20th and early 21st century less specificity characterizes the Ivy League student in popular culture but these students are implicitly represented as individuals who have made it, who have achieved something special, whose experience is "more special" than that of other students at anonymous universities. As discussed in the third chapter, the importance of the Ivy League schools as part of "national memory" (Thelin, 2011, p. 1) continues to bolster their importance and that of the students within them. All of which provides interesting fodder for plots that illustrate students or their families doing anything to belong to such an institution (e.g., *Harvard Man*, 2001; *Orange County*, 2002; *Risky Business*, 1983; *Soul Man*, 1986; *Stealing Harvard*, 2002) (Conklin, 2008). Alternatively, the students taking distance education or correspondence courses, or attending propriety schools, junior colleges, and community colleges, bear the stigma of "losers" in fiction (Pittman, 1988, 1992). As the dean of students in the pilot of the TV show *Community* explains,

> *What is community college? Well, you've heard all kinds of things. You've heard it's 'loser' college for remedial teens, 20-something dropouts, middle-aged divorcees, and old people keeping their*

minds active while they circle the drain of eternity. That's what you've heard. [Pumping arm in air.] I wish you luck!

Perhaps part of the distinction reserved for Ivy League institutions relates to gender and the Ivy League's late coeducationalization in comparison with other institution types. Despite the overwhelming male representation of college students in popular culture, fictions that depict community colleges present a different student face to their audiences. The dominant student in these fictions are nontraditional women, called "reentry students," "runaway housewives," and "weepers" (LaPaglia, 1994). Rather than pursuing college for their own benefit, these fictional women often enter community college to help their families by increasing their employability but can be punished in the narratives for their presumption to step out of their "place." LaPaglia (1994) claims that the overall tone describing community college students, even as the image diversifies to include more groups than just the "runaway housewife," is one of mockery and identification with the "loser" label. Students' identification with institutional type provides powerful messages about privilege, inclusion, and exclusion.

Institutions and Their Students

Polarizing and hierarchical notions of worth aligned with institution and student types provide many opportunities for (mis)education. Illustrated throughout this section, belonging is a key theme of college student portrayal in popular culture. Institutional identity and academic year featured prominently in the purported identity of popular culture students and certain institutions still benefit from portrayals indicating that attendance there means something of distinction for the students.

Related to these observations about the portrayal of college students is the increasing importance of the notion of popularity throughout 20th-century popular culture. The following section discusses how smaller group identity supersedes academic class or institutional identity influencing perceptions of hierarchy and individuality in the (mis)educating representations of college students.

Popularity and Privilege in College Student Popular Culture

Categorizing and defining different types of college students present in popular culture revolves around changing notions of the popular and different avenues for distinction, individuality, and notoriety within collegiate life. Types of college students appear to be more about youth culture and the value of higher education in general than complex commentary about college students themselves. Examining how these types work in popular culture provides an interesting lens when examined temporally and exposes a shifting negotiation in college student identity and popularity that examines aspects of belonging, gender, and college participation as primers for (mis)education.

Belonging to "U"

A defining feature of college student identity revolves around belonging. How well students belong contributes to their popularity in the texts but what they must identify themselves with changes, particularly throughout the later end of the 20th century and the beginning of the 21st century. In the late 19th and early 20th centuries, student identity is subsumed by institutional delineations such as class rank and college of choice as indicated previously. Later identity messages in popular culture diffuses the importance of institutional demarcations (except for Ivy League schools) moving more toward individual traits as shown in Figure 5.

The necessity of belonging showed college students defined by others rather than self with their worth indicated through participation in activities and groups. Greeks and Jocks, for example, tend toward presentations of a popular, desirable class of students and the Grinds or Nerds receive less worthy portrayals. Earlier artifacts in the late 19th and throughout the 20th century explicitly reinforced these definitions of popularity. Narratives admired

FIGURE 5
Identity Traits and Shifting Locus of Status

Prior to and early 20th century:	**INSTITUTION** ←→	Individual
From later in the 20th century:	Institution ←→	**INDIVIDUAL**

the athletic heroes, extolling the deeds and characters of those admitted to their ranks (Messenger, 1981). Thinking about the safe/scary depictions discussed in the third chapter, it seems that shifting to a more individualistic and differentiated portrayal of college students accompanies the shift to scarier institutions. This also supplements the increase in the visibility of representation of different institutional types. Institutions become more anonymous as the students gain more importance and as students become more differentiated, the importance of institutional affiliation minimized except for certain cultural artifacts focusing on predominantly Ivy League institutions.

Popular culture plays with, challenges, and reinforces notions of popularity among fictional college students. Early college films showed awkward characters played by Harold Lloyd and Buster Keaton trying to be accepted through participation in sporting events in their attempts to win the girl (Bilton, 2008). This theme continues later in the century with *Revenge of the Nerds* (1984) most explicitly challenging the notion of the popular by pitting the nerds against the nasty jocks. In the early 21st century, popular culture rhetoric continuing from high school narratives such as *High School Musical* (2006), *Mean Girls* (2004), and *Glee* (2009–) proffered messages about breaking down barriers between cliques, not labeling self, and limiting opportunity. The unpopular becomes popular with narratives displaying characters who "own" labels that previously were uncool such as nerd and geek to confidently enhance their popularity.

We Belong to "U" Too

Akin to the depiction of institutions, portrayals that veer away from a White, male, straight portrayal of higher education move from complete invisibility, to select visibility, before achieving wider but token representation in popular culture. Less research focuses on groups of students distinct from straight, White males but pieces that do exist provide important insight about the ways that other characters belong in college popular culture artifacts.

Women Students. In early fictional depictions of college women, female students attending women's colleges are uniformly termed "college girls" in magazines, news stories, and popular culture artifacts (Marchalonis, 1995). Early women's fiction focused on women's colleges explicitly and implicitly challenges this unilabel presenting college women as individuals with different skills, perspectives, abilities, talents, and purposes for attending higher education. Women in these colleges are part of a community and the fiction displays multiple labels for the nature of a college women as "shark," "dig," "grind," "all-round girl," "the beauty," and "butterflies." Some of these terms are familiar from Horowitz's (1988) work and the student types in Table 7 earlier in this chapter, but most important in Marchalonis's (1995) analysis is the idea of gaining "prominence" for college women at women's colleges particularly in the Progressive Era. In contrast to this notion of individuality, Inness (1995) counters this argument with the idea of interchangeability, that the women college student characters and by projection, college women themselves, should be interchangeable in values, appearance, purpose, and choices. The prominent theme of borrowing in the women's college novels of the Progressive Era provides one example of interchangeability. Inness interprets students borrowing from one another in college novels as acts that emphasize who belong due to their ability to lend material goods. Essentially, the exemplary college girl is a student explicitly related to a comfortable social-economic status where acts that suggest agency may be interpreted as economic displays, as privileged spectacle (Inness, 1995). Indeed Clark (1998) describes an example of this in advertisements from the late 1940s where college women's upper-class and sophisticated depiction, what Clark describes as her "polished sensibilities rather than her intellectual abilities" (p. 188), is used to market bras, luggage labels, and other goods.

Women's college narratives provided an idyllic foundation for the portrayal of students, one which failed to cross boundaries to depictions of women in other institutions. Unfortunately women's literature focused on coeducational institutions present female students by 1920s as "intruders" (Marchalonis, 1995). Later in the 20th century, TV narratives also emphasize that women students are not the norm by portraying their engagement in nontraditional ways and/or in feminized or care-related disciplines. Education is the major of choice for some of the few TV female students mentioned by Dalton and Linder (2008) such as *Funny Face* (1971) and *Eight is Enough* (1977–1981). *Funny Face* (1971) features a working female student who is an education major at UCLA. A female graduate student pursues a PhD in child psychology (*Party of 5*, 1994–2000) but her work is feminized not only through her scholarly focus on children but also through her choice of work to support her studies as a nanny and the narrative focus of the show on relationships (Dalton & Linder, 2008). Alternatively, women law students study law at an elite institution in *The Paper Chase* (1978–1986) but until the late 1990s and 2000s it's more common for the TV portrayals with female students to portray nontraditional students (e.g., *Gertrude Berg Show*, 1961–1962; *Eight is Enough*, 1977–1981; *Pearl*, 1996–1997; *That's Life*, 2000–2002) than elite or traditional students. Twenty-first century TV provides more shows that focus on women students at coeducational institutions (e.g., *Felicity*, 1998–2002; *Gilmore Girls*, 2000–2007; *Veronica Mars*, 2004–2007; *Greek*, 2007–2011; *Community*, 2009–) but again men dominate the total roles, the choices made by women characters, and narrative rationales despite lead female characters. The lead protagonist Felicity in the TV show of the same name even chooses her college by following a man from high school after he momentarily notices her on high school graduation day. Twenty-first century movies also reinforce college women's diminished importance through narratives that are "anti-singlehood and anti-independence" (Yakaboski & Donahoo, 2012, p. 17).

TV programming portrays graduate as well as undergraduate female students but despite this variability, which arguably indicates that women have the ability, access, and opportunity to pursue graduate work, narrative choices undermine the competency of female graduate students (Byers, 1996). Allegations and findings of plagiarism in her dissertation damage the achievements and opportunities of the female child psychologist in *Party of 5* (1994–2000) (Dalton & Linder, 2008), and a female PhD mathematician in *Numb3rs* (2005–2010) chooses the possibility of a relationship with her former advisor over a good career opportunity elsewhere. A graduate student in *Beverly Hills, 90210* cheats on her professor husband with the unwitting Brandon, and then attempts to seduce another wealthy character to fund her PhD research (Byers, 2005). Popular culture (mis)educates viewers/consumers through the portrayal of hysteric and grotesque female graduate students (Byers, 1996) who cheat, restrict opportunity, and lie (Dalton & Linder, 2008).

Race and Sexuality. In *Beverly Hills, 90210* viewers' exposure to racial and sexual diversity occurs by way of a jack-in-the-box strategy for its narrative; token characters pop up for a short time for a specific narrative purpose and are then boxed away out of sight of the viewer and remain absent from continued participation in the broader narrative (Byers, 2005). The 2000s follows this jack-in-the-box strategy from 1990s mainstream TV shows, such as *Beverly Hills, 90210,* with token stability, where diverse characters remain a constant in the narrative rather than serving to educate the other characters (and viewers) at discrete plot moments. For example, *Felicity* (1998–2002) and later *Greek* (2007–2011) both have major characters throughout the series who are African American. Elena played by Tangi Miller is Felicity's competitor, friend, and roommate. She brings racially diverse male college students into the show through her romantic relationships with Blair and later Tracy. Calvin and Ashley are African American friends of the major White characters in *Greek* (2007–2011), and Calvin is also a gay Black man, coming out early during the first season to the main character, Rusty. Race is never a salient part of the narrative in *Greek* but Calvin's sexuality does provide narrative intrigue throughout the show. Although a main character in *Greek* is gay, sexual diversity remains closeted in popular culture representation in general. S. Vilardo (personal communication, March 5, 2014) observes that lesbian sexual identity is particularly maligned in college portrayals that treat students' lesbian identity as something temporary, as an experiment or a vacation from heteronormativity (e.g., *Greek*, 2007–2011; *Sorority Boys*, 2002). Indeed, Yakaboski and Donahoo (2012) observe how some film narratives "stigmatize and devalue the lesbian identity" (p. 12) by discounting women's sexual agency.

The racial diversity of college students remains limited in popular culture with African American presence far more prominent than that of other non-White racial or ethnic groups, featuring in all-Black cast movies, Black magazines, newspaper articles, and reality TV set at HBCUs. Beyond African American cultural texts, there continues to be very little broader racial inclusion both in media texts and in the literature about the texts related to portrayal of college students. Latinos/as, American Indians, and Asian characters as college students remain rare, token or isolated in media, reminiscent of Lalo Guerrero's 1986 comic song "No Chicanos on TV" (Venegas, 2012). As Guerrero states,

I think that I shall never see, any Chicanos on TV. Huggies has
their three babies: Black and White and Japanese. Chicano babies
also pee, but you don't see them on TV.

Chicanos also go to college which is another representation you rarely see on
TV (Venegas, 2012).

Media with major characters and storylines focused on non-White,
straight characters explore the differentiation within these communities, moving beyond the perceived homogeneity of tokenism to a depiction of more
complex communities. Cousins (2005) analyzes the representation of Black
students attending an HBCU and a state university in the movies *School
Daze* (1988) and *Higher Learning* (1995). These films portray conflicts within
the Black community in general, between those going to college and those
not, between Black characters within university, as well as between Black and
specifically White characters. Through moments of understanding and mis-
understanding, conflict and cohesion, these films provide a reductionist but
privileged perspective that exposes a differentiated depiction of characters
from the Black community and their relationship to higher education, rather
than one mediated through a White gaze (Cousins, 2005). Additionally, Speed
(2001) contends that these films and *House Party 2* (1991) illustrate social con-
straints faced by African Americans through the portrayal of behavioral over-
policing, presumptions of criminal activity, and the salience of poor backgrounds evidenced in these films. College film tries to "reconcile" these issues through the portrayal of fun activities and hedonistic expressions (Speed,
2001).

In an analysis of TV shows featuring HBCUs, Parrott-Sheffer (2008) describes the fictional Hillman College in *A Different World* (1987–1993) as
distinguished by conservative family values and the students' ability to help
one another regardless of friendships. This show of family values is contrasted
with the more recent depiction of African American students at HBCUs in
the first two seasons of *College Hill* (2004–2007), a reality TV show set at
different campuses. The author reports that the director wanted to focus on
HBCU students due to their first-generation status and their overwhelming honesty. Although this reality show portrays sensationalized depictions of

HBCU students, it is interesting that both shows had a foundation in wholesomeness, in the honesty of *College Hill*'s mostly low SES students and the conservatism of the Hillman College environment.

In contrast to purposeful HBCUs on TV, Au (2005) examines what he terms "rap music's discursive battle with education" (p. 210). His analysis claims that Kanye West's *College Dropout* (2004) belongs to rap's "economic battle" with higher education as West posits that higher education isn't worth the money and implies it has no point for African Americans; for West, social mobility is an illusion that college cannot dispel (Au, 2005). Richardson's (2011) analysis of *College Dropout*, in addition to West's later work *Late Registration* (2005) and *Graduation* (2007), adds to this work considering West's critique of higher education as linked with Bourdieu's ideas of education and reproduction.

Limited research considers women and particularly students of color in popular culture reflecting the inadequate depiction of a wider demographic of students. Despite women's sustained strength in enrollment and graduation numbers, male overrepresentation appears to outnumber women's success. The token representation of race and sexual diversity in popular culture college texts is scarcely considered in research literature. These limited and token portrayals of women and students from diverse populations bear huge potential for (mis)education particularly for answers to questions about who belongs; it could seem that only straight, White men truly belong in higher education.

Gendered "U"

Popular culture college students enact gendered norms, performing, challenging, and reinforcing salient or alternative characteristics of gender in cultural artifacts sometimes in ways that bolster male privilege (Byers, 2005). Although feminist and queer theorists might argue that gender performance is more complex than rendered here, in the context of this monograph representations of institutional type, single-sex societies, and college activities all provide ways to perform gender in exaggerated ways that limit, oppress, marginalize, champion, or privilege the characters.

FIGURE 6
Shifting Masculinities of Popular Culture College Men

| Pre-mid-20th century: | **HEGEMONIC** | ←→ | hyper | ←→ | alternative |
| Post-mid-20th century: | **HEGEMONIC** | ←→ | HYPER | ←→ | alternative |

The portrayal of male students expressed in popular culture across the period examined for this monograph depicts shifting negotiations and performances of masculinity (see Figure 6; Bilton, 2008; Tucciarone, 2007a). These range from universal depictions of hegemonic masculinity where patriarchy and traditional roles, such as the idea of the male breadwinner, hold sway, to hypermasculinity where ideals embedded in hegemonic masculinity, for example, leadership, action, risk, adventure, competition, and privilege become subverted to aggressive and perhaps hedonistic versions of the former ideal. These manifest through risky behaviors, such as excess drinking, drug use, unprotected sex, casual sex, and the objectification of women in college narratives. Alternative masculinities challenge perceptions of what it means to be a man in a number of ways: by defying heteronormativity, substituting competition with collaboration, and finding value and worth in ways without relying on the dominance of women and the appearance of physical strength. Indeed analysis of news media suggests dominant perspectives placing male students as victims of women's successful presence in higher education (Yakaboski, 2011).

Figure 6 visualizes the ongoing dominance of hegemonic masculinity in college representations while showing the presence of hyper and alternative masculinities. In the pre-mid-20th century hypermasculine portrayals occur as do the rare alternative identities but in the post-mid-20th century hypermasculine portrayal rival hegemonic depictions and alternative models of masculinity have a greater presence than in the pre-mid-20th century but still less prominent in overall representation.

Just going to college aligns with hegemonic expectations of men but female college students' attendance challenges social norms of femininity. Popular culture with women college students explicitly or implicitly explores this quandary from the late 1800s to the present (Donahoo & Yakaboski, 2012;

FIGURE 7
Shifting Notions of Femininity Represented by Sexual Activity

| Pre-mid-20th century: | **VIRGINAL** | ←→ | sexualized |
| Post-mid-20th century: | virginal | ←→ | **SEXUALIZED** |

Inness, 1993, 1994, 1995; LaPaglia, 1994; Marchalonis, 1995; Reynolds & Mendez, 2012; Yakaboski & Donahoo, 2012). Some of the roles and characteristics of feminine women include: caretaking, deferring, and being empathetic, attractive, and meek. In many ways these qualities resonate with aspects of changing portrayals of college women's sexual activity in popular culture, particularly in movies and TV where women gained more conflicted portrayals regarding responsibility for their own sexual choices from mid-20th century (see Figure 7). It is interesting to note that in early fiction college men's (hetero)sexual adventures in college novels were not with college women but with nonstudents, although Lyons (1962) mentions that in Stone's sensational *Pageant of Youth* (1933) a coed "seduced 107 men in less than a semester" (p. 76).

Aligned with the safe and scary institutional spaces in the third chapter, as female students increasingly challenge hegemonic and patriarchal expectations through actual college attendance, engagement, and success, a parallel phenomenon occurs where portrayals of college women shift from characters who are safe, secure, and looked after to vulnerable, potential victims. Higher education popular culture becomes a dangerous place for female college students in the late 20th century. Women are sexually coerced, raped, assaulted, stalked, and kidnapped in *Beverly Hills, 90210* to emphasize their femininity and their need to be rescued (Charlebois, 2012) presumably despite their audacity to attend college at all. Byers (2005) describes the *90210* college women as willing to "lie, cheat, steal, and use sex to get what they want" (p. 80) in ploys that negatively obscure and use traditional spheres of femininity as a foil to obtain power. Alternatively, despite the dangers of higher education for women in certain media and artifacts, some movies with college women also align with the typology of fairy tales, depicting metaphorical princesses in films from 2000 to 2008 who battle evil queens and find their princes (Donahoo & Yakaboski, 2012). College women face narrative punishment or continued marginalization through implicit or explicit traditional role replication in these characterizations.

Greek life and athletics both provide avenues for the negotiation of gender in college-related popular culture for both male and female characters. Portrayals of Greek life provide hegemonic, mostly heteronormative single-sex environments providing male students the opportunity to break rules, risk discovery, objectify women, and party, becoming increasingly hypermasculinized in portrayals throughout the 20th century (Speed, 2001). In an extreme depiction, a fraternity is even displayed as being at the service of a demon in *Buffy the Vampire Slayer* (Wilcox, 1999). For women, Greek life provides opportunities to challenge certain aspects of femininity. Greek women increasingly exhibit some of the same behaviors as men through their sexual activity and socializing. However, in ABC Family's *Greek*, the behaviors and choices of the women may have changed from earlier fictional portrayals of sorority women but the values and expectations underlying the text remain those attributed to women by Welter (1966, p. 152) in 1820–1860 as pure, domestic, and submissive women (Reynolds & Mendez, 2012).

College sport provides the ultimate expression of hegemonic masculinity in popular culture. In novels of the 1890s eulogizing the sports hero, football provides an outlet for college men to be a "beast" or "brute" (Messenger, 1981, p. 148). Particularly, football provided opportunities for male students to demonstrate their leadership, physical prowess, and competitive spirit (Miller, 2010). Messenger (1981) distinguishes college sportsmen in novels from young people who aren't college students delineating between "popular sports heroes" and "school sports heroes" where college sportsmen (and only men in his analysis) work toward victories that go beyond self-aggrandizement and reward. College sportsmen distinguish themselves from noncollege sportsmen through their pursuit of self-discipline with collegiate athletics acting as a passport for democratic fellowship and future involvement in capitalistic enterprises (p. 156).

From 1890 to 1915, magazines portrayed college as *the* place to forge the ideal middle-class man through fiction and advertisements, written and designed mostly by a variety of alumni, related to college sports (Clark, 2010). Clark (2010) declares that, "The athletic contest instilled all of the essential features of self-made manhood—toughness, courage under fire, perseverance, and (of course) character" (p. 116). According to Messenger (1981), male collegiate athletes at the end of the 19th century engaged in a battle between good and evil where novels used metaphors of war to elevate the heroic actions of the young men fighting for their college on the field. From the end of the 1920s until WWII, these representations shift from group unity ideals to those of a more individualized nature where, in football movie narratives, sport is a crucible that hones players so that college sport becomes a metaphor for men's lives that was particularly powerful during this period of between war depression (Miller, 2010). Miller (2010) claims that these films promote "an ideology that often masks social problems by suggesting that if individuals can gain control over their own bodies they can gain control over their own economic and social destiny" (p. 1223). In an era in which football players in films increasingly included characters from working class and ethnically diverse backgrounds, this type of narrative promoted class and ethnic promises of a work-hard meritocracy as people from different backgrounds were thrust together in layered competition for footballing success, heterosexual conquests, and winning the big game. More recent depictions of male students move away from sports being related to virtue, community, and leadership for men, and instead focus on "hyper-masculinized behavior" (p. 38) that objectifies and demeans women as a source of heterosexist male-bonding and community (Bindig, 2008). Alternative narratives continue the theme of victory from adversity and the importance of community either based on historical events (e.g., *We Are Marshall*, 2008) and/or underdog narratives (e.g., *Rudy*, 1993).

Similar to male students, athletics for female college students is salient in popular culture mostly around the turn of the 20th century. Unlike the male students, investment in narratives about women's sport do not continue throughout the 20th century with few examples of college women and sports in popular culture in comparison with those for men's college sports other than the airing of actual games. Even in televised actual games female athletes remain gendered through broadcast commentary describing their attractiveness, physical attributes, and their prowess as "pretty" (e.g., Billings, Halone, & Denham, 2002). College women's sports teams have little post-mid-20th century representation; in fact, a dog plays in a team sport in the movies (*Airbud*, 1997) before a film focused on a team of college women. *Love and Basketball* (2002) features a female college basketball player but the first fictional movie to focus solely on college women's sport depicts a historical example of a women's college basketball team in *The Mighty Macs* (2011). Based on real events, women at a small Catholic school fight against notions of femininity, poor facilities, lack of resources, and recalcitrant administrators to become champions in this underdog movie.

In contrast with the absence of women's sport in popular culture from the mid-20th century, analysis of early women's college fiction describes athletics as a way for women students to "subvert" prescriptions of femininity in the college novel (Inness, 1993). In various novels, Inness (1993) reveals a battle between gymnastics and competitive athletics for college women where gymnastics was a way to isolate women, and focus on the individual's deficits that needed improvement for increased attractiveness for men, ability to bear children, and constitution for housework. She describes how the women's college novel pushes back by advocating for vigorous enjoyment in team sport and spectatorship. Through sport, community engagement becomes more important rather than individual prowess, with individuals contributing to the whole rather than solely individual, something that can be taken from the court or playing field to life beyond college (Smith, 1977).

The gendered "U" of popular culture presents accentuated versions of (mis)educating normative conceptualizations of masculinity and femininity particularly through narratives that feature collegiate sports and Greek life. Gender is closely linked in popular culture and media representations from the mid-19th century to the present with sexuality, expectations, and behaviors that remain implicitly or explicitly affirmed or challenged.

Social Versus Academic "U"

An important facet of (mis)education concerns popular culture's necessary focus on the social aspects of students' college life. U.S. movies and TV shows largely aim to entertain rather than edify the viewer, while other media aims for both in varying degrees and artifacts. The desire to entertain combined with a unique American anti-intellectualism leads to more focus on college experience rather than academic adventures (Hinton, 1994). Conklin (2008) suggests that this lack of attention reflects the actual division of time real students spend on academics. His observation includes students in the early 1900s who worked to be average as well as some students in the 20th century who use college as a privileged time to avoid and delay adult responsibilities, as a "time out" to grow into an adult identity without supervision. So too is the higher education of popular culture a privileged time to transition into adult, gendered, class roles in historical texts or for some to enjoy a time out in late 20th- and early 21st-century texts. Possibilities for (mis)education due to narrative choices focusing on the social bear great significance for viewers or consumers of popular culture artifacts and their subsequent impressions and beliefs related to students' actual participation in higher education and what that engagement means for their social success in college.

Concessions to students' academic lives in popular culture include depictions of students going to class, cramming for a test, or working in the library but they are rarely portrayed actually engaged in their work. Sociology students in Conklin's (2009) work focus on relationships, and have variable representation related to intellectual endeavor and acumen. In general, romantic relationships provide a mainstay for plot choices in novels, movies, and TV shows (Byers, 2005; Conklin, 2008; Lyons, 1962; Umphlett, 1984; Yakaboski & Donahoo, 2012). Cartoons and comic strips provide a more pointed gaze on student life satirically skewering students' interaction with professors, advisors, parents, their engagement in college, and college preparedness (e.g., Kelly, 2009; http://www.alternateuniversity.com). Pertinently, Mackey (2003) claims that the prominence of fictional students' frustration with academics reduces the voices of students who find joy in this work as exemplified by some of the students in the TV show *Felicity* (1998–2002).

Academics provide a foil for student individuation either as a community in early artifacts or for individuals in more contemporary representations where wiz-kids or geeks gain acceptance when their skills find a use to further the aims of the social. In the ABC Family TV show *Greek* (2007–2011), for example, Rusty, the polymer science protagonist, who desperately seeks what he calls a "real college experience" through participation in a fraternity, finds acceptance and notoriety when he steals an NSF-funded project and makes it rain beer at a party (Reynolds & Mendez, 2009).

Knowledge of a student's major is usually only offered in narratives to propel the plot. Experimentation with differing rituals and ethical standards encountered in a classics education provides the foundations for events in Tartt's (1992) bestselling *The Secret History* and Cappie's undecided major status in *Greek* (2007–2011) means the writers pull on a variety of knowledge gleaned from short stints in numerous majors as a way for his character to explain love and life to his mentee in a variety of amusing ways.

When in the classroom, student portrayal revolves around three staples: boredom, rebellion, or, albeit rarely, inspiration. Manifestations of boredom in narratives where students sleep through class or lack any engagement reinforce students' social prerogative in popular culture as well as (mis)educating regarding the teaching skills of professors, expectations of professorial style, and the utility of higher education. Challenging professorial authority occurs in texts from the late 1800s to the present as a way to exercise student determinism (Lyons, 1962; Reynolds, 2009; Reynolds & Mendez, 2009; Ryan & Townsend, 2010). Inspiration is often represented by a passive student response illustrating examples of good teaching through "sage on the stage" performances rather than compelling demonstrations of student learning or engagement.

Narratives sabotage academic engagement in situations where students place more effort toward avoiding the work necessary to succeed in their classes by cheating instead of preparing. Although Progressive Era women college stories present cheating as something completely unacceptable to the college and student peers (Inness, 1995; Lindgren, 2005; Marchalonis, 1995), by the 1990s moving from the portrayal of undergraduate women to a graduate student, TV presents a female graduate student who plagiarizes in her dissertation (Dalton & Linder, 2008). Progressive Era men cheat with abandon and without consequences in college novels (Inness, 1995; Lindgren, 2005; Lyons, 1962; Messenger, 1981) and in 21st-century TV Rusty and most of his fraternity brothers cheat on their exams in *Greek*. However, advanced women students are portrayed as knowing through cheating, as unable to present their own understanding of the texts, get caught, and face consequences unlike the male students. Interestingly, White male students are presented as not needing to "know" academically to be successful. *Animal House* (1978) illustrates the epitome of this claim in the epilogue for the film, which tracks the post-college success of these masochistic, hedonistic slobs.

Rote knowledge and trivia, which can be remembered and regurgitated, rather than research or creativity, is extolled through popular culture in the various game shows that feature contestants from college or reward contestants with a scholarship to go to college. Examples of these shows include college editions of *Jeopardy*, as well as the radio and various TV versions of *College Bowl*, plus the British show *University Challenge*, a university game show that was the subject of a movie starring James McAvoy, *Starter for 10* (2006). Ryan and Townsend (2010) also discern a preference for the factual in the portrayal of students in the 1950s where the portrayal of students at all levels, including college, shows students seeking specific factual answers to their queries from instructors, never engaging in intellectual pondering or creative thinking (p. 50). This tension is specifically encountered in *Mona Lisa Smile* (2003), where Wellesley's new art teacher challenges the students to move beyond their memorization of facts to understand, discuss, and critique art (Hamdan, 2005). Popular culture presents trivia expertise as a commodity for students to exploit in these media while academic engagement is positioned as useless in postgraduation films where students struggle to find jobs and question the worth of their degrees and majors (Conklin, 2008). The alliance of these shows with college also potentially (mis)educates viewers about the purpose of college to one about rote learning and remembering instead of exploring, thinking, questioning, and creating.

Despite occasional depictions of academics, the majority of college student portrayals focuses on the social and presents it as the raison d'etre for college life. The gaze of projected traditionally aged students suggests that institutions of higher education are places where students apply little effort or time to academics, where finding people "like you" is vital in a space dedicated to the evasion of responsibilities. Media focused on nontraditional students bring different values to their engagement in and expectations of their time in higher education such as Tom Hanks character in *Larry Crowne* (2011), other community college characters in fiction (LaPaglia, 1994), or veteran students in movies and novels of the 1940s and 1950s (Pittman & Osborn, 2000). Veteran students from World War II invest so much in their fictional education that Pittman and Osborn (2000) describe their characterization as "paragons of scholarly virtue" (p. 22). This is epitomized by Norman Rockwell's illustration of his recurring subject "Willie Gillis" as a studious veteran on the cover of the Saturday Post in 1946 (Clark, 1998). Different periods and media display students' control of and expectations for the relationship between academics and the social in their college experiences in culturally relevant and institutionally specific ways.

Narratives display student experience through varying explorations in hedonistic activities. This is true of older as well as more recent artifacts. Hevel (2014) examines the role of alcohol in the depiction of college students in novels from 1865–1933. He finds that in earlier novels drinking is associated with male bonding, exceptionalism, and urbanity. The use of alcohol in the texts distinguishes who belongs, especially for men in Ivy League institutions. Nineteenth-century novels also dealt with issues to do with college students and town prostitutes, and Lyons (1962) describes early 20th-century novels such as *This Side of Paradise* (1920) and *The Plastic Age* (1924) as writing about "amoral experiments" (p. 76), and Stone's *Pageant of Youth* (1933) as a "catalogue of sex and violence" (p. 76). Even movies of the 1930s and 1940s dealt with topics such as a student seducing a town girl (*The Age of Consent*, 1932) and a male student attempting to rape a female professor (*The Accused*, 1949). The difference between older and more recent cultural artifacts often lies in the levels of explicit description or depiction. In *The Age of Consent*, the audience sees the student go into the town girl's house at night and sees him there the next morning whereas more contemporary artifacts might also include a sex scene rather than rely on editorial suggestion and dialogue. Twenty-first century media portrays the college party scene and related explorations with sex, drugs, and alcohol in films (e.g., *Van Wilder: Freshman Year*, 2009), TV shows (e.g., *Blue Mountain State*, 2010–2011), and music (e.g., Asher Roth's 2009 single *I Love College*). Membership with Greek or athletic organizations provides access to the party scene but those students not part of these groups also experiment and indulge. An interesting contrast with students' experimentation is that they are also positioned as teachers for their professors (Keroes, 2005) but these teachings relate to moral rather than academic subject matter. Indeed, Byers (2005) describes students of *Beverly Hills, 90210* as the "moral guardians" (p. 77) of their professors. Navigating moral boundaries and individual choices demonstrates a narrative manifestation of the self-important world of students where thinking everyone is against you other than your circle turns out to be true in an institution where students have reduced power despite their privilege.

In popular culture, the ideal students are social joiners. They join teams, organizations, and parties; they belong. Miller (2010) claims that the glut of college sports films between 1925 and 1940 served to reinforce the social rather than the academic in cinematic portrayals of college life with their reliance on narratives that fused romance with athletic challenge and achievement. It could be argued that popular culture students' contribution to the academy manifests mostly as one derived through athletics (Inness, 1993; Miller, 2010).

In the battle between the social and the academic, elitism and privilege emerge as a clear fascination in cultural texts (Hinton, 1994), either through institutional selectivity, athletic prowess, or admittance to select campus groups, like Greek life and secret societies (e.g., *The Skulls*, 2000). Popular culture simultaneously extols and challenges selective student societies, mixing a desire to belong and hope for the future with plots that ethically query what people are willing to do to be noticed, to belong, to succeed that has little to do with the academic purpose of institutions of higher education.

Other than Greek life and athletics, extracurricular campus activities of students such as student government or the student newspaper are minimized in film (Conklin, 2008). TV's *Gilmore Girls* (2000–2007) offers one glimpse into extracurricular activities through costar Rory's involvement with the Yale student newspaper. Overall, student contribution for maintaining their learning environment becomes subverted by the pursuit of pleasure. In contemporary film and TV, the student gaze in a subgenre of college texts often renders institutions of higher education as places where young people roll from one party and one partner to the next (e.g., *Blue Mountain State*, 2010–2011) at mega parties where it even rains beer (e.g., *Greek*, 2007–2011), and alumni wish they could return to such ways (e.g., *Old School*, 2003). This wish is even expressed in the song "I wish I could go back to college" in the Broadway hit puppet musical, *Avenue Q* (2003), as a time when "life was much simpler" and you could "f*ck your TA."

The social versus academics in popular culture produces heavy-handed, misleading, and nostalgic versions of college life for mass (mis)education. Understanding and deconstructing the impetus for such an imbalance is vital to understand the distorted expectations applicants, students, and parents have of college life.

Concluding Thoughts

Popular culture's college students embody numerous opportunities for (mis)education related to their demographics and engagement in higher education. Despite the increasing inclusion of students of color, women, and people with differing sexualities, White, straight men still dominate representation in the early 21st century. This is a particularly pertinent candidate for (mis)education considering the increased presence and success of women in higher education, one that is not meaningfully reflected in cultural texts. Limited representations of people of color and differing sexualities also (mis)educate consumers about opportunity and access to higher education for people from a variety of backgrounds. Ultimately, popular culture provides limited templates for college student engagement and behavior in college that exemplify extreme standards for gender performance and belonging that place notions of self-worth and social worth in potential competition. Students' engagement in popular culture's higher education revolves around and enacts privilege that commodifies higher education through the focus on the social and the minimization of the academic.

(Re)educating "U": Learning From Popular Culture

Introduction

G ROWING UP IN 1980s Britain my Dad used to watch the BBC children's show *Grange Hill* (1978–2008) with me. This show was set at a comprehensive secondary school and addressed major educational and social issues as part of its storyline. The students also often got up to no good, hence its popularity with young people. As the head teacher of a school my Dad said he watched the show (or asked me about the episode) to "find out what's going to happen tomorrow." Students would often copy the antics in the storylines at school (and presumably in schools across Britain) but after watching or hearing about the show my Dad could give teachers a heads-up about certain issues or instructions to watch out for particular behaviors to try to proactively prepare for and avoid dangerous or disruptive situations in class and on the grounds at school.

My advocacy for popular culture research in higher education stems from these early observations of one of my Dad's professional practice strategies in a certain period of his career. He didn't give up learning about students from professional sources but after repeated experiences with students where they admitted to doing something because they'd seen it in this TV show he supplemented his preparation for school safety and discipline with a popular culture source.

Numerous studies in communication studies, sociology, and psychology show that popular culture artifacts influence behavior, attitudes, values, beliefs, and the choices of people (e.g., Allen et al., 1995; Anderson et al., 2003, 2010; Bleakley et al., 2008; Gomillion & Giuliano, 2011; Huesmann et al., 2003; Jernigan et al., 2005; Russell et al., 2009; Signorielli, 2010; Taylor, 2005; Villani, 2001; Ward & Friedman, 2006). Therefore, popular culture that focuses on the people or setting of higher education provide templates for viewers/readers/consumers to form opinions and beliefs about them which subsequently influence their discourse and action in or toward higher education. Although admittedly few in number, scholars who have approached popular culture with higher education questions in effects-research substantiate this hypothesis, showing that popular culture does influence the perceptions and behavior of students (Tobolowsky, 2001; Tucciarone, 2007b; Wasylkiw & Currie, 2012). For example, Wasylkiw and Currie (2012) found that negativity toward academics and positivity toward drug use increased with college students who watched *Animal House* (1978). Institutional reports from Marshall University and Immaculata University also describe an increase in applicants after the films *We Are Marshall* (2006) and *Mighty Macs* (2011) were screened. Although both these movies used past institutional events as the inspiration for their narratives, these fictional depictions had the same impact on admissions as the boost actual sporting team success notoriously places upon admissions numbers (Pope & Pope, 2009; Toma & Cross, 1998). The focus of this chapter discusses how major themes emerging in my analysis of the existing literature contribute toward (mis)education as well as ideas for use of popular culture research to contribute to (re)education, before concluding with suggestions for future research utilizing popular culture texts as sources for research.

It seems a small leap to suggest that popular culture influences more than institutional enrollment but through its (mis)educative power extends expectations for experience, templates for behavior, substitutes for self-knowledge, and guides for values to affect consumers explicitly and implicitly. In addition to direct effects, popular culture provides scholars with sources to explore, reveal, and challenge dominant and alternate (Polan, 1986) meanings related to higher education. Revealing these meanings offers faculty, practitioners, and administrators additional and varied understandings for the ways that those inside and outside the academy act toward and interact with higher education.

Opportunities for (Re)education

The idea of (re)education takes for granted the reflective, proactive professional engagement of faculty, administrators, and practitioners in higher education. It acknowledges the explicit and implicit messages of popular culture and in doing so provides a new script, alternative voices, to redress power and claim agency for institutions and the people in them. For me, the idea of (re)education, despite its totalitarian ring, is about voice and the imperative of professionals within institutions to define their worth and work, to inclusively determine who belongs and who succeeds. These efforts reside in critical, ongoing appraisals of our organization(s), considerations about role and value, and evaluations of the ways we market and present ourselves in *knowing* opposition to or collusion with the messages of (mis)education.

The Dominance of Straight White Males

Some might think that this major theme is unsurprising, but it is nevertheless important and worth revealing, especially because this observation concerning White male privilege is not a general statement regarding patriarchy or hegemonic masculinity in U.S. society or U.S. popular culture in general. Neither is it a statement about the past; it is an observation about continued, persistent, and dominant portrayals where straight, White male privilege is repeatedly reinforced. From the mid-1800s to early 21st-century existing research demonstrates that straight White men dominate all roles in popular culture's representation of higher education as students, faculty, and administrators; higher education belongs to heterosexual White men. Despite expressed media concerns about women's involvement in higher education hurting men as explored by Yakaboski (2011), young men receive numerous and repeated tacit messages about higher education being their place, their playground. Hypermasculinized representations reinforce existing privileges suggesting that as part of a privileged group, young, straight White men need not work or worry about the future being able to focus on the immediacy of college as a pleasurable present.

Considering these portrayals, analyses of popular culture reinforce the need for professionals to pay attention to straight White men at college in ways that counter the hypermasculine messages repeatedly expressed in popular culture narratives, particularly later 20th- and 21st-century TV and movies. Young men are bombarded with images and narratives providing templates for behavior that encourage hypermasculinity in college exemplified by hedonistic and misogynistic performances. These behaviors valorize the social and condemn the academic but popular culture representation repeatedly alludes to the after-college success of mediocre and academically disengaged straight, White male students (e.g., *Animal House*, 1978; *Sorority Boys*, 2002). As popular culture influences choices, behaviors, and values, administrators and practitioners can use the templates of behavior exhibited in popular culture as opportunities for young men to consider "what it means to be a (college) man" through collaboration between student affairs and academic affairs. Opportunities to assess and evaluate male identity can occur through programming in a variety of venues including: orientation, residential halls, Greek life and athletics, diversity and gender initiatives, as well as academic programming related to specific courses, living-learning options, and first-year seminars. Programs that provide straight White men opportunities to identify their expectations for behavior and examine their foundations acknowledges the identity development of young people in ways that recognize the explicit templates they are given for performance of a college student identity.

Popular culture research, among others, reminds straight White male faculty, administrators, and practitioners to be aware of their own privilege in the academy and to recognize their overrepresentation in popular culture. (Re)education for this group of professionals involves recognizing straight, White male overrepresentation, noting differences and even deference in interaction as opposed to other colleagues not meeting these demographical markers. The dominance of this group of men in popular culture stresses the need for advocacy as a professional trait where straight, White men act as explicit advocates for dispelling attitudes and beliefs regarding role, rank, and markers of difference.

Translating popular culture research to practice requires that straight, White male professionals in the academy challenge privilege while simultaneously being conscious of their own privilege and the potential influence of popular culture messages on themselves. For example, athletic coaches for male team sports, faculty and practitioner advisors for all-male social groups, faculty in male-dominated disciplines, and others should use this research as inspiration to be advocates to dispel locker room or group disparagement of difference by not participating in and condoning privileged derision through active but educative rebuttal.

Several implications for marketing and institutional representation arise related to this theme. Marketing efforts can revolve around the perceived desirability of (straight White) male enrollment especially when one considers the prominence of marketing linked with male sporting events (Tobolowsky & Lowery, 2006) and materials that cater to formats deemed most appealing to men in color and content. These choices appear to institutionally condone the representation of higher education as a place for men, particularly straight, White men, contributing to a narrow conceptualization of the contemporary college man.

Popular culture repeatedly tells young straight, White men that college is their place yet still institutions also make choices reinforcing this message to specifically tell these students "this institution is your place" with little attempt to lure other demographics of students. Although worrying gaps between race and class remain, it is interesting that the gender gap is only of concern when more women clamor to enter higher education in greater numbers than men, despite steady increases in the overall numbers of men attending college (King, 2006, 2010; Ross et al., 2012). Institutions should carefully consider why they want to appeal to male applicants and critically appraise if marketing choices reinforce straight White male privilege in higher education in ways that are antithetical to contemporary and institutional collegial values. Just because the film industry considers its market to be young men of a certain age does not mean that institutions of higher education should follow this practice.

The Missing and the Token

The reverse of the dominance of straight White men in higher education, this theme exposes the missing, minimized, and tokenized portrayals of other people as characters in higher education. Student, faculty, and administrators of color, women, and homosexual characters are among those missing as main protagonists. The missing, minimized, and tokenized also include: working students; students involved in activities other than Greek life or sports; more recently, veterans; Latino/as; first-generation students; disabled students; low SES students; students who are parents; commuter students; and others. For faculty, the missing includes faculty of certain disciplines (e.g., languages and business) as well as minimizing or tokenizing faculty and administrators with different demographic profiles. The barren representation of administrators and practitioners in higher education excludes the broad and necessary role that both sets of professionals play in the life, success, and running of an institution. The (mis)education of popular culture omits their presence and function ignoring the hoards of professional responsibilities maintained by administrative positions.

These missing characters contribute to a worryingly homogenous portrayal of higher education, one that institutions have made efforts to move away from in actuality. The missing, minimized, and tokenized in popular culture send strong and persistent (mis)educating messages about institutional options, who belongs in higher education, and what people do in higher education. (Re)education involves using these observations from popular culture research to examine ways in which the academy also reproduces the (mis)education of popular culture to exclude and limit the potential and presence of a diverse institutional population.

Popular culture underrepresents the diversity of actual students, faculty, administrators, and practitioners on campus. Research about these omissions can inspire professionals in the academy to ascertain if institutions themselves also minimize difference even while contemporarily touting the importance of it. One strategy for professionals rising from this research involves assessing the visual depictions of institutions to discover who is shown as belonging. This not only includes websites and marketing materials but also pictures, banners, and art on campus. When we enter the main administration building of our campuses, for example, we glean messages about who is valued and who belongs from the presentation of faces on the wall. These faces are usually White male faces due to institutional histories and the way they naturally mirror sociocultural limitations concerning race and gender. Institutions should attempt to balance the historical legacy of a White male campus through prominent and authentic recognition of changed and changing demographics that are not limited to certain spaces, such as a multicultural or women's center, but pervade the campus. I am not advocating that we forget our institutional histories but suggest we balance these with other visuals in an attempt to enact discourses of inclusivity with demonstrations of diverse worth. Institutions can find ways to move beyond or complement recognition of the legacy of former administrators with depictions of everyday and exceptional events, moments, and people that demonstrate our institutions' desire to make visible the invisible and find the missing without tokenizing either.

In addition to the missing people of higher education, another concern revealed in the research relates to missing roles in popular culture representations. Tobolowsky (2006) mentioned that missing administrators in TV portrayals of higher education could be a disadvantage for students who learn about what higher education is and how to engage in it through cultural texts. I repeat this concern after reviewing existing literature and noticing the limited opportunities to provide positive templates for administrative function, role, and interaction across media and genre. Interaction with administrators is often adversarial in texts, which could condition students, and even faculty, to expect conflict and opposition from people in these roles. Due to the missing representation of administrators and practitioners, professionals can use this revelation from popular culture research as an imperative for (re)education by considering and implementing different strategies to introduce students to those who work in higher education. For example, as professors often get questions about issues they cannot help with, all syllabi for 100/200-level courses could include a section of contact information for common, noncourse FAQs. Due to the ubiquitous presence of mobile platforms among the student body, another strategy could be to develop an institutional "app" that lets students ask questions; the app could simply tell them who or what office to contact. Finally, sections of orientations could stress the variety of roles and functions of practitioners and administrators ready to assist students in their institutions. These three ideas help reveal and promote popular higher education's missing professionals to actual college students.

Marketing efforts for institutions should be careful to not be swayed by the (mis)education of popular culture and make authentic and innovative attempts to present an inclusive institution. The limited portrayals of students in popular higher education could deter some from enrolling or discourage others from engaging in certain disciplines. Professionals should assess the content of websites and admissions materials and determine who is represented as belonging in these media. If institutional media conforms to the overrepresentation of straight, White men and underrepresentation of diverse members of academic communities in all roles, efforts should be made to authentically redress the balance of representation for faculty and students considering discipline and the distribution of types of engagement. For example, African American students should not only be represented through engagement with a Black Student Union or other like groups, and women should not be solely portrayed in social groups of women. Authenticity is key in institutional representation, balancing the reality of underrepresentation with the value of and welcome for increased participation. The analysis of academic pictures also should consider depictions of power and privilege. For example, do group pictures of students around a computer seemingly depict male students showing female students what to do? These are just a few perspectives to assess materials based on how popular culture research reveals (mis)educating messages that institutions themselves may be guilty of perpetuating.

The Salience of Institutional Type

The huge influence of institutional types for the (mis)educating power of popular culture came as a surprise as part of this review, but the salience of this theme cannot be denied across the literature. This bears noting particularly for institutional types that are invisible, anonymous, or value-decimated in popular culture. Community colleges and the people in them bear the brunt of cultural disdain while elite institutions receive repeated, named reinforcements of superiority and privilege. Institutional depiction clearly illustrates (mis)educating messages concerning who belongs and importantly who does not belong at these institutions. The (mis)education allied to these depictions potentially influences student choice, college choice advice, and even impressions of who belongs for administrators responsible for admissions considerations. Notions of belonging and worth also interact interestingly with the varying visibilities of women's colleges and HBCUs.

Importantly, the salience of institutional type's contribution to (mis)education intimately entwines with the prior themes of White, straight male dominance and the missing. Despite the increasing engagement of diverse students, faculty, administrators, and practitioners in higher education, the distorted focus on certain institutional types and the (mis)educating messages about them present limited conceptualizations of U.S. higher education that decry the vibrant diversity of institutional types and the essential service they all provide.

(Mis)educating messages about institutional type distort value and role for institutions' civic mission but institutions can use popular culture media as part of (re)educating strategies to inform counter messages and counter practice. Faculty, administrators, and practitioners should be aware of the ways popular culture depicts institutional types, particularly their own type of institution. Being fully aware of and understanding these messages allows professionals to recognize when others inside and outside the institution reproduce these messages or act in accordance with these messages. Professionals at institutions could evaluate how common messages about institutional type revealed through popular culture research influence their own choices and values, asking if institutions and the people in them have been conditioned by the messages of popular culture to conform to low expectations or distorted representations instead of fighting against them. This type of work can lead institutions to engage in a process that considers institutional identity related to type not only organizational culture in ways that could encourage and excite professionals who work there. It can also lead to a plan to fight against, to counter the (mis)educating messages related to institutional type for specific institutions. This could be important for recruiting and hiring professionals in all roles, as well as for developing partnerships outside of the academy.

Institutions can use popular culture media to advertise their institutions and attempt to generate name recognition that can be of use to the institution, just like Harvard and other Ivy League institutions benefit from repeated name recognition in popular culture representations. Despite Parrott-Sheffer's (2008) discomfort with the representations of HBCUs in *College Hill* (2004–2007), he claims that the show's contribution to name recognition benefited the institutions involved through increased applications and enrollments. As part of entrepreneurial leadership, institutions could seek media representations in new markets, could pursue, pitch, and use media involvement rather than avoid representation. For example, depending on the storyline, perhaps institutions used as a setting for movies could negotiate the use of the name of their institution with production companies. People look up fictional institutions online like *Monsters University*'s fake college webpage related to the film of the same name and the TV show *Community*'s fake website for Greendale Community College. Use of university names as part of TV shows or films could increase website traffic for institutions with the fictional representations being a gateway for first contact.

Another strategy to use media to benefit from the name recognition garnered through popular culture texts could involve a competition on campus to write a script focused on a narrative featuring and set at your own institution for a movie or play. Real-life stories about college inspire narratives like *The Great Debaters* (2007), *Kinsey* (2004), *We are Marshall* (2006), and *Mighty Macs* (2011). Whether inspired by scandal, success, celebration, or controversy, institutions of higher education must all have one great story waiting to be told, if not several. Perhaps senior administrators could arrange for the winning script(s) to be sent to production companies or TV networks for consideration. Essentially this idea, or others like it, is built on the premise of trying to find ways to manufacture opportunities for name recognition more widely to approach the name recognition that some institutions have never had to work for but undeniably benefit from.

Marketing for institutions balance a tension between selling an experience and setting people expect in higher education with the need to differentiate from the masses. Regarding institutional type and dispelling subsequent (mis)education, marketing could actually use (mis)education from media to advertise type. For example, a community college could work against negative messages in popular culture by using the popularity of the TV show *Community*. A billboard or advertisement could use the picture of a character from the show that said, "If I lived closer to an Ivy Tech Community College[2] campus, I'd go there!" Other community colleges could use Jay Leno's negativity to their advantage. For example, "Comedians like to joke about community colleges but do you think we're a joke?" This question would be preceded by a list of notable facts about the institution, and its name. Additionally, invisible institutions like a women's college could satirically embrace the "scary feminist" rhetoric in popular culture, playing with shared meanings offered through popular culture texts to amuse, engage, wryly acknowledge, and counter the negativity related to these aspects of (mis)education.

Knowing popular culture research findings related to institutional type allows professionals in the academy to identify what is expected of their institution, to differentiate themselves from other institutions in the way they align or differ from common messages, and to use the (mis)education of popular culture for their own advantage.

Academic-Lite Higher Education

The marginalization of academics, the academically invested, and even, at times, the research of faculty, is an ongoing feature of popular culture (mis)education that dangerously undermines and distorts the purpose of higher education. Cultural templates that posit institutions as bastions for parties, sports, and petty in-fighting diminish the important foundation of college existence. The minimization of academics is a disturbing and potentially dangerous aspect of the (mis)education of popular higher education. If academics are not important then college is only about college life, therefore reducing the meaning and value of higher education to a social experience rather than a formal education. Academic-lite representations of higher education insidiously denigrate the importance of an educated citizenry, and deteriorate the integrity and worth of the academic enterprise. Repeated narratives reinforce the tangential and nonessential importance of academics as part of the college experience that has possible repercussions for the work of professionals in the academy to inside and outside constituencies.

Major issues in the academy could be interpreted as instigated or reinforced by the (mis)education of popular culture. These include: the challenged value of a liberal education; the prominence of and desire for professional and applied disciplines; the intolerance for more obscure fields; political contempt for aspects of social science research; state mandates attempting to manage professorial work; escalating divisions between administration and faculty; the decrease in full-time faculty and increase in part-time faculty; among other issues.

Limiting the role of academics impacts faculty, students, administrators, and practitioners. For faculty, this (mis)education minimizes the importance of faculty role, diminishes the value of expertise, and questions the use of faculty research discerned through analysis of faculty and discipline portrayals. For students, the academic-lite portrayal distorts expectations concerning their preparation, attendance, and participation for classes, as well as investment in projects, papers, and examinations. It leads to perceptions that college is about the social and supports behaviors that diminish the academic contributing to the "I learned more outside class than in it" rhetoric. Academic-lite portrayals also impact administrators and practitioners who receive the same messages about faculty and students that may influence their professional choices and behaviors in ways that reinforce the unimportance of academics and the faculty involved with them.

Challenging academic-lite representations is imperative for higher education professionals. A major (re)educating endeavor should involve the image of institutional faculty in ways that delineate institutional contribution and the worth of their work beyond the classroom. As popular higher education research shows faculty as misunderstood, strategies to bolster the academic function of an institution could include initiatives to humanize and personalize academics, as well as celebrate academic work. For example, websites could include short video blogs for "A Day in the Life of a Professor" that feature professors from different disciplines, while academic success should be as widely touted as sports success. Celebrating academic success should be a given but this can be hidden or taken for granted in institutional media and attitudes. If institutions show that academics are important, we can (re)educate and counter academic-lite narratives.

Research about popular higher education should inspire administrators and practitioners to assess their own values and beliefs about faculty work and responsibilities. A professional development session that allows professionals to reflect on faculty work and the importance of academics in an institution could reveal the influence of (mis)education and opportunities for (re)education in the ways that faculty are taken for granted, where assumptions of importance are espoused without specifics, or even how faculty are obstacles instead of partners for institutional success.

Prospective and new students apply to and enter our institutions with expectations influenced by popular culture narratives. Due to the academic-lite nature of representation institutions should engineer opportunities for explicit and engaging communication about academics in application materials, campus tours, advertisements, orientation, first-year seminars, and student life programming.

Finally, professionals on campus should assess the visual images on and/or about campus to determine if these conform to social norms about the representation of higher education as academic-lite. For example, some of the questions that could be considered in this assessment include: In what way are institutions portrayed on their webpages? What pictures or videos are suggestive about or explicitly engage in academic work? Are academic images minimized? What activities dominate materials, images, and media about your institution? Do social endeavors eclipse academic endeavors? Are faculty and faculty work highlighted in engaging ways? Does your institution identify with academics or highlight social/situational attributes? These and many other questions could reveal opportunities to change institutional co-optation of an academic-lite narrative.

(Re)education requires assessment, reflection, and a commitment to change for those already working in higher education and for projections of institutional identity. How popular higher education is represented provides important information about power, privilege, inclusion, and exclusion related to perceptions and norms about the academy, that institutions also unknowingly reproduce. Popular culture research focused on higher education supplements existing research about academia, providing additional perspectives that urge a wider focus on and responsibility for institutional image and perception. Further research focusing on popular higher education can add to and refine understanding for action concerning the themes revealed as part of this review as well as others.

Future Popular Culture Research

So little research exists from the discipline of higher education that multiple possibilities abound for topics and questions examining popular culture artifacts. Scholarship could focus on the people and institutions of higher education or explicitly examine the major themes emerging from this review, as well as delineating issues, challenges, topics, and areas of interest from the field. Future research should continue to reveal the shared and alternate meanings regarding higher education and its characters while also assessing the effects of these messages on behaviors and beliefs. This research should focus on a variety of media and an assortment of genres considering the influence of media and genre upon portrayals and the opportunities for and power of (mis)education. Based on this review and existing research, the following suggestions provide broad topics for future research that would complement and add to existing research in ways that would benefit higher education and student affairs professionals.

Studies should examine the major emergent themes of this review to explore their veracity in different periods, medias, and genres. For example, the portrayal of straight White men offers opportunities for research examining masculinity, hypermasculinity, and male identity development while research considering the missing and token makes the invisible visible. This research also advocates for increasing recognition of higher education's inclusivity while exposing areas of exclusion and exclusivity that systemically, institutionally, and organizationally exist. Numerous questions and approaches await examination concerning gender, sexuality, race, and class in popular higher education. For example, how is sexuality portrayed in and across higher education texts? One opportunity in this area involves analyzing texts like *Greek* (2007–2011), *Sorority Boys* (2002), and *Dawson's Creek* (1998–2003) to examine depictions of (homo)sexuality and Greek life.

Further work should also focus on the other main themes revealed in this review. More in-depth work examining depictions of institutional types could add to understanding about popular perceptions of different institutions to assist campus teams in using, rebutting, or confirming norms associated with type. Additional work could examine institutional types with little or no existing research concerning their representation in cultural texts, such as military institutions, minority-serving institutions, and religious institutions. Finally, examining the role of academics in popular culture could determine the ways in which academics are minimized and contribute toward increased academic agency in institutional branding and self-identification.

In addition to bouncing off the themes discerned as part of this review, scholars should explore popular higher education representation aligned with features and topics explicitly important to professionals in higher education. For example, what can we learn about popular culture's (mis)education related to finance, access, college choice, college preparation, student involvement, identity development, depictions of drinking and parties, faculty roles, administrative roles, and numerous other topics? Researchers can concentrate on different roles of people within higher education, and free different demographical portrayals from obscurity and invisibility by focusing on their few representations. Studies with more unusual foci could provide a range of perspectives on student life, such as the depiction of students' first days, roommate relationships, portrayals of college spaces, and representations of collegiate community. Other work could focus on particular groups, for example, analyzing Greek life and athletic portrayals to discern the unique aspects of these subgroups and what shared meanings related to these groups suggest about higher education. Similar to Gasman's (2007) and Yakaboski's (2011) work, scholars can trace important events, issues, or higher education people in news media or examine the rhetoric linked with higher education in political propaganda and debates. For example, in what ways did/do major newspapers discuss Title IX? What common and alternative ideas about higher education dominate televised presidential debates?

Finally, in addition to research concentrating on U.S. cultural texts, there is potential for international and comparative work to study popular higher education. Other countries also produce texts that represent higher education in their nations. British literature teems with examples and India produces many college novels and films. As well as determining that which is distinct about international popular higher education, scholars can compare with U.S. texts, for example, comparing the first-year experience of students in British universities through analysis of TV shows (e.g., *Off the Hook*, 2009–; *Fresh*

Meat, 2011–) with U.S. shows (e.g., *Greek*, 2007–2011; *Undeclared*, 2001–2003).

These are just a few broad examples of the options for research examining higher education popular culture and media. Hopefully continued work in this exciting and nascent part of the field of higher education continues to critique the (mis)education of popular culture representation in ways that reveal messages regarding inclusion and exclusion so that institutions can use these insights to welcome the popularly excluded, expose institutional conformity with norms revealed in popular culture, and claim agency through (re)educating strategies.

Conclusion

Higher education popular culture in the United States is a powerful and persistent phenomenon portraying images and narratives that extol and demean, limit and exaggerate features of institutions that influence ideas about actual higher education. This review revealed that a dominant imagining of higher education presents a White, male, straight, wealthy, distinguished, and social academy, unwelcoming of difference, and contemptible of the new. This explicit and implicit lack of inclusivity and the valorization of exclusivity in popular higher education should be a huge concern for the academy. The (mis)education of popular higher education presents popular condemnation for our institutions and/or popular desires for exclusivity that institutions should challenge. Most of all I believe existing work in this area, plus the possibilities of future research, present exciting opportunities to build bridges between expectations and realities, creating opportunities to espouse our agency by crafting institutions and experiences that go beyond (mis)educating messages about them.

Hopefully this monograph illustrates that these cultural texts bear significance for scholars and professionals in higher education. (Mis)education is real but (re)education is also possible if scholars and professionals take the opportunity to learn more about the (mis)education of popular higher education and attempt to use their understandings for the betterment of our institutions, and people's experiences with them.

Notes

1. See http://comicbookplus.com for copies of these and other comics out of copyright.
2. Ivy Tech Community College is the name of Indiana's community college system.

References

Allen, M., D'Alessio, D., & Brezgel, K. (1995). A meta-analysis summarizing the effects of pornography II: Aggression after exposure. *Human Communication Research, 22*(2), 258–283.

Anderson, C. A., Berkowitz, L., Donnerstein, E., Huesmann, L. R., Johnson, J. D., Linz, D., … Wartella, E. (2003). The influence of media violence on youth. *Psychological Science in the Public Interest, 4*(3), 81–110.

Anderson, C. A., Shibuya, A., Ihori, N., Swing, E. L., Bushman, B. J., Sakamoto, A., … Saleem, M. (2010). Violent video game effects on aggression, empathy, and prosocial behavior in eastern and western countries: A meta-analytic review. *Psychological Bulletin, 136*(2), 151–173.

Anderson, C. K., & Clark, D. A. (2012). Imagining Harvard: Changing visions of Harvard in fiction, 1890–1940. *American Educational History Journal, 39*(1/2), 181–199.

Anderson, C. K., & Thelin, J. R. (2009). Campus life revealed: Tracking down the rich resources of American collegiate fiction. *The Journal of Higher Education, 80*(1), 106–113.

Andreeva, N. (2013, August 16). Fox nabs comedy from '30 Rock's Matt Hubbard, Tina Fey & Robert Carlock and Universal TV with series commitment. *Deadline.* Retrieved from http://www.deadline.com/2013/08/fox-nabs-comedy-from-30-rocks-matt-hubbard-tina -fey-robert-carlock-and-universal-tv-with-series-commitment/

Araujo, J. (2012). *"This is college. You only live once": The portrayal of college sorority women in horror films.* Unpublished manuscript.

Archer, D. E., Stewart, H. L., Kennedy, K., & Lowery, J. W. (2011, March). *For mature audiences only: Greek life in horror film.* Session presented at the 2011 College Student Educators International—ACPA Annual Conference, Baltimore, MD.

Armstrong, G. B., & Neuendorf, K. A. (1992). TV entertainment, news, and racial perceptions of college students. *Journal of Communication, 42*(3), 153–176.

Au, W. (2005). Fresh out of school: Rap music's discursive battle with education. *The Journal of Negro Education, 74*(3), 210–220.

Ball, P. (2006). Chemistry and power in recent American fiction. *HYLE—International Journal for Philosophy of Chemistry, 12*(1), 45–66.

Bauer, D. M. (1998). Indecent proposals: Teachers in the movies. *College English, 60*(3), 301–317.

Bevan, D. (Ed.). (1990). *University fiction* (Vol. 5). Atlanta, GA: Rodopi.

Billings, A. C., Halone, K. K., & Denham, B. E. (2002). "Man, that was a pretty shot": An analysis of gendered broadcast commentary surrounding the 2000 men's and women's NCAA Final Four basketball championships. *Mass Communication and Society, 5*(3), 295–315.

Bilton, A. (2008). Hot cats and big men of campus: From this side of paradise to the freshman. *European Journal of American Culture, 27*(2), 93–110.

Bindig, L. (2008). *Dawson's Creek: A critical understanding*. Lanham, MD: Lexington Books.

Bjorklund, D. (2001). Sociologists as characters in twentieth-century novels. *The American Sociologist, 32*(4), 23–41.

Bleakley, A., Hennessy, M., Fishbein, M., & Jordan, A. (2008). It works both ways: The relationship between exposure to sexual content in the media and adolescent sexual behavior. *Media Psychology, 11*(4), 443–461.

Bode, C. (1950). Hawthorne's Fanshawe: The promising of greatness. *New England Quarterly, 23*(2), 235–242.

Bosco, M. (2007). John L'Heureux's 'The Handmaid of Desire': Desiring the good academic imagination. In M. Bosco & K. Connor (Eds.), *Academic novels as satire: Critical studies of an emerging genre* (pp. 131–145). Lewiston, NY: Edwin Mellen Press.

Britt, T. R., & Tunagur, U. (2011). Imagined realities: Appalachia, Arabia, and Orientalism in *Songcatcher* and *The Sheik*. In A. B. Leiter (Ed.), *Southerners on film: Essays on Hollywood portrayals since the 1970s* (pp. 161–174). Jefferson, NC: McFarland & Company.

Brooks Bouson, J. (2007). 'Teaching English isn't the clean work it used to be': Satirizing the plight of token professionals in Richard Russo's *Straight Man*. In K. R. Connor, M. Bosco, & S. J. Lewiston (Eds.), *Academic novels as satire: Critical studies of an emerging genre* (pp. 111–130). Lewiston, NY: Edwin Mellen Press.

Byers, M. (1996). Constructing divas in the academy: Why the female graduate student emerges in prime-time television culture. *Higher Education Perspectives, 1*, 99–118.

Byers, M. (2005). Those happy golden years: *Beverly Hills, 90210*, college style. In S. Edgerton, G. Holm, T. Daspit, & P. Farber (Eds.), *Imagining the academy: Higher education and popular culture* (pp. 67–88). New York, NY: RoutledgeFalmer.

Campbell, A. (2005). Women, sport, and film class. *Women's Studies Quarterly, 33*(1/2), 210–223.

Campbell, N. D., Rogers, T. M., & Finney, R. Z. (2007). Evidence of television exposure effects in AP top 25 college football rankings. *Journal of Sports Economics, 8*(4), 425–434.

Carens, T. L. (2010). Serpents in the garden: English professors in contemporary film and television. *College English, 73*(1), 9–27.

Cham, J. (1997–). *Piled higher and deeper*. Retrieved from http://phdcomics.com/comics.php

Chambers, J. (2006). Presenting the Black middle class: John H. Johnson and Ebony Magazine, 1945–1974. In D. Bell & J. Hollows (Eds.), *Historicizing lifestyle: Mediating taste, consumption and identity from the 1900s to 1970s* (pp. 54–69). Burlington, VT: Ashgate.

Charlebois, J. (2012). *The construction of masculinities and femininities in Beverly Hills, 90210*. Lanham, MD: University Press of America.

Clark, D. A. (1998). "The two Joes meet. Joe College, Joe Veteran": The GI bill, college education, and postwar American culture. *History of Education Quarterly, 38*(2), 165–189.

Clark, D. A. (2010). *Creating the college man: American mass magazines and middle-class manhood, 1890–1915*. Madison: University of Wisconsin Press.

Clifford, D., Anderson, J., Auld, G., & Champ, J. (2009). Good Grubbin': Impact of a TV cooking show for college students living off campus. *Journal of Nutrition Education and Behavior, 41*(3), 194–200.

Conklin, J. E. (2008). *Campus life in the movies: A critical survey from the silent era to the present.* Jefferson, NC: McFarland and Company.

Conklin, J. E. (2009). Sociology in Hollywood films. *The American Sociologist, 40*(3), 198–213.

Cousins, L. H. (2005). Black higher learnin': Black popular culture and the politics of higher education. In S. Edgerton, G. Holm, T. Daspit, & P. Farber (Eds.), *Imagining the academy: Higher education and popular culture* (pp. 247–266). New York, NY: RoutledgeFalmer.

Crockett, S. A., Jr. (2013, June 14). White students at Black colleges: What does it mean for HBCUs? *The Washington Post.* Retrieved from http://www.washingtonpost.com /local/therootdc/white-students-at-black-colleges-what-does-it-mean-for-hbcus/2013/06 /14/a60e1afa-d4f5-11e2-b05f-3ea3f0e7bb5a_story.html

Crowley, J. N. (1994). *No equal in the world: An interpretation of the academic presidency.* Reno: University of Nevada Press.

Dagaz, M., & Harger, B. (2011). Race, gender, and research: Implications for teaching from depictions of professors in popular film, 1985–2005. *Teaching Sociology, 39*(3), 274–289.

Dalton, M. M. (2007). *The Hollywood curriculum: Teachers in the movies* (Revised ed.). New York, NY: Peter Lang Publishing.

Dalton, M. M., & Linder, L. R. (2008). *Teacher TV: Sixty years of teachers on television.* New York, NY: Peter Lang Publishing.

Daspit, T., & Weaver, J. A. (2005). Rap (in) the academy: Academic work, education, and cultural studies. In S. Edgerton, G. Holm, T. Daspit, & P. Farber (Eds.), *Imagining the academy: Higher education and popular culture* (pp. 89–114). New York, NY: RoutledgeFalmer.

Day, D. (1997). *A treasure hard to attain: Images of archaeology in popular film, with a filmography.* Langham, MD: Scarecrow Press.

DeGenaro, W. (2006). Community colleges, the media, and the rhetoric of inevitability. *Community College Journal of Research and Practice, 30*(7), 529–545.

DeMoss, S. (2012). *The exclusivity of the Ivy League: An analysis of Harvard student profiles and images in popular culture—Implications for higher education.* Unpublished manuscript.

Donahoo, S., & Yakaboski, T. (2012, November). *Classifying coeds: Typologies of college women in the movies.* Paper presented at the annual meeting of Association for the Study of Higher Education (ASHE), Las Vegas, NV.

Elena, A. (1997). Skirts in the lab: Madame Curie and the image of the woman scientist in the feature film. *Public Understanding of Science, 6*(3), 269–278.

Engle, J., & Tinto, V. (2008). *Moving beyond access: College success for low-income, first-generation students.* Washington, DC: Pell Institute for the Study of Opportunity in Higher Education.

Farber, P., & Holm, G. (2005). Selling the dream of higher education: Marketing images of university life. In S. Edgerton, G. Holm, T. Daspit, & P. Farber (Eds.), *Imagining the academy: Higher education and popular culture* (pp. 117–130). New York, NY: RoutledgeFalmer.

Flicker, E. (2003). Between brains and breasts—Women scientists in fiction film: On the marginalization and sexualization of scientific competence. *Public Understanding of Science, 12*(3), 307–318.

Franzini, A. R. (2008). Is school cool? Representations of academics and intelligence on teen television. In L. Holderman (Ed.), *Common sense: Intelligence as presented on popular television* (pp. 187–198). Lanham, MD: Lexington Books.

Gasman, M. (2007). Truth, generalizations, and stigmas: An analysis of the media's coverage of Morris Brown College and Black colleges overall. *Review of Black Political Economy, 34*(2), 111–135.

Gerbner, G. (1987). Science on television: How it affects public conceptions. *Issues in Science and Technology, 3*(3), 109–115.

Giroux, H. (2009). Cultural studies, critical pedagogy, and the politics of higher education. In R. Hammer & D. Kellner (Eds.), *Media/Cultural studies: Critical approaches* (pp. 88–106). New York, NY: Peter Lang Publishing.

Glazer-Raymo, J. (2001). *Shattering the myths: Women in academe.* Baltimore, MD: Johns Hopkins University Press.

Glazer-Raymo, J. (2008). *Unfinished agendas: New and continuing gender challenges in higher education.* Baltimore, MD: Johns Hopkins University Press.

Goldberg, L. (2014, January 24). Margaret Cho to co-star in Fox's Tina Fey comedy (exclusive). *Hollywood Reporter.* Retrieved from http://www.hollywoodreporter.com/live -feed/margaret-cho-star-foxs-tina-673901

Gomillion, S. C., & Giuliano, T. A. (2011). The influence of media role models on gay, lesbian, and bisexual identity. *Journal of Homosexuality, 58*(3), 330–354.

Gordon, L. D. (1987). The Gibson girl goes to college: Popular culture and women's higher education in the progressive era, 1890–1920. *American Quarterly, 39*(2), 211–230.

Gramsci, A. (1971). *Selections from the prison notebooks of Antonio Gramsci* (G. Nowell-Smith & Q. Hoare, Eds. & Trans.). New York, NY: International Publishers.

Hall, M. A. (2004). Romancing the stones: Archaeology in popular cinema. *European Journal of Archaeology, 7*(2), 159–176.

Hall, S. (1997). *Representation: Cultural representations and signifying practices.* Thousand Oaks, CA: Sage.

Hamdan, A. (2005). "Mona Lisa Smile": More than a smile [Film review]. *International Education Journal, 6*(3), 417–420.

Hark, I. R. (2004). Crazy like a prof: Mad science and the transgressions of the rational. In M. Pomerance (Ed.), *Bad: Infamy, darkness, evil, and slime on screen* (pp. 301–314). Albany: State University of New York Press.

Harris, A. (2009). The good teacher: Images of teachers in popular culture. *English Drama Media, 14,* 11–18.

Hawlitschka, K. (2003). Sunrooms, Starbucks, and salmon steak: Academic nonsense and domestic sensibility in Lev Raphael's Nick Hoffman mysteries. *The Journal of American Culture, 26*(1), 96–103.

Haynes, R. (2003). From alchemy to artificial intelligence: Stereotypes of the scientist in Western literature. *Public Understanding of Science, 12*(3), 243–253.

Haynes, R. (2006). The alchemist in fiction: The master narrative. *HYLE—International Journal for Philosophy of Chemistry, 12*(1), 5–29.

Hevel, M. S. (2014). Setting the stage for Animal House: Student drinking in college novels, 1865–1933. *Journal of Higher Education, 85*(3), 370–401.

Hinton, D. (1994). *Celluloid ivy: Higher education in the movies 1960–1990*. Metuchen, NJ: The Scarecrow Press.

Holtorf, C. (2007). *Archaeology is a brand!: The meaning of archaeology in contemporary popular culture*. Oxford, UK: Archaeopress.

Horowitz, H. (1988). *Campus life: Undergraduate cultures from the end of the eighteenth century to the resent*. Chicago, IL: University of Chicago Press.

Huesmann, L. R., Moise-Titus, J., Podolski, C. L., & Eron, L. D. (2003). Longitudinal relations between children's exposure to TV violence and their aggressive and violent behavior in young adulthood: 1977–1992. *Developmental Psychology, 39*(2), 201–221.

Ikenberry, S. (2005). Education for fun and profit: Traditions of popular college fiction in the United States, 1875–1945. In S. Edgerton, G. Holm, T. Daspit, & P. Farber (Eds.), *Imagining the academy: Higher education and popular culture* (pp. 51–66). New York, NY: RoutledgeFalmer.

Inness, S. A. (1993). "It is pluck but is it sense?": Athletic student culture in progressive era girls' college fiction. *The Journal of Popular Culture, 27*(1), 99–124.

Inness, S. A. (1994). Mashes, smashes, crushes, and raves: Woman-to-woman relationships in popular women's college fiction, 1895–1915. *NWSA Journal, 6*(1), 48–68.

Inness, S. A. (1995). *Intimate communities: Representation and social transformation in women's college fiction, 1895–1910*. Madison, WI: Bowling Green State University Popular Press.

Jaschik, S. (2005, June, 2). Community colleges to Jay Leno: Shut up. *Inside Higher Ed*. Retrieved from http://insidehighered.com/news/2005/06/02/leno

Jernigan, D. H., Ostroff, J., & Ross, C. (2005). Alcohol advertising and youth: A measured approach. *Journal of Public Health Policy, 26*(3), 312–327.

Jiwani, Y. (2005). The Eurasian female hero[ine]: Sydney Fox as Relic Hunter. *Journal of Popular Film and Television, 32*(4), 182–191.

Kahlenberg, S. (2008). Book, street, and techno smarts: The representation of intelligence on prime-time television. In L. Holderman (Ed.), *Common sense: Intelligence as presented on popular television* (pp. 107–140). Lanham, MD: Lexington Books.

Kanter, M. J. (2011). American higher education: "First in the world." *Change: The Magazine of Higher Learning, 43*(3), 7–19.

Kellner, D. (2009). Towards a critical media/cultural studies. In R. Hammer & D. Kellner (Eds.), *Media/cultural studies: Critical approaches* (pp. 5–24). New York, NY: Peter Lang Publishing.

Kelly, F. (2009). Supervision satirized: Fictional narratives of student-supervisor relationships. *Arts and Humanities in Higher Education, 8*(3), 368–384.

Keroes, J. (2005). Picturing institutions: Intellectual work as gift and commodity in *Good Will Hunting*. In S. Edgerton, G. Holm, T. Daspit, & P. Farber (Eds.), *Imagining the academy: Higher education and popular culture* (pp. 39–50). New York, NY: RoutledgeFalmer.

King, J. (2006). *Gender equity in higher education: 2006*. Washington, DC: American Council on Education Center for Policy Analysis.

King, J. (2010). *Gender equity in higher education: 2010*. Washington, DC: American Council on Education.

Kramer, J. E. (1979). Images of sociology and sociologists in fiction. *Contemporary Sociology: A Journal of Reviews, 8*(3), 356–362.

Kramer, J. E. (1981). College and university presidents in fiction. *Journal of Higher Education, 52*(1), 81–95.

Kramer, J. E. (1999). The American college mystery: An interpretative history. In P. Nover (Ed.), *The great good place? A collection of essays on American and British college mystery novels* (pp. 1–14). New York, NY: Peter Lang Publishing.

Kramer, J. E. (2000). *College mystery novels: An annotated bibliography.* Lanham, MD: Scarecrow Press.

Kramer, J. E. (2004). *The American college novel: An annotated bibliography* (2nd ed.). Lanham, MD: Scarecrow Press.

LaPaglia, N. (1994). *Storytellers: The American college novel: An annotated bibliography. The image of the two-year college in American fiction and in women's journals.* Dekalb, IL: Leps Press.

Leuschner, E. (2006). Body damage: Dis-figuring the academic in academic fiction. *Review of Education, Pedagogy, and Cultural Studies, 28*(3/4), 339–354.

Lindgren, G. (2005). *Higher education for girls in North American college fiction 1886–1912* (Vol. 110). Lund, Sweden: Lund University Press.

Litton, J. A. (1996). The Sweet Valley High gang goes to college. *The Alan Review, 24*(1). Retrieved from http://scholar.lib.vt.edu/ejournals/ALAN/fall96/f96-06-Litton.html

Louie, V. S. (2004). *Compelled to excel: Immigration, education, and opportunity among Chinese Americans.* Stanford, CA: Stanford University Press.

Lowe, M. (2003). *Looking good: College women and body-image, 1875–1930.* Baltimore, MD: Johns Hopkins University Press.

Lucas, C. J. (1994). *American higher education: A history.* New York, NY: St. Martin's Press.

Lyons, J. O. (1962). *The college novel in America.* Carbondale: Southern Illinois University Press.

Mackey, M. (2003). Television and the teenage literate: Discourses of "Felicity." *College English, 65*(4), 389–410. Retrieved from http://www.jstor.org/stable/3594241

Maier, S. (1999). The scholar as detective: The literary life of Carolyn G. Heilbrun as Amanda Cross's Kate Fansler. In P. Nover (Ed.), *The great good place? A collection of essays on American and British college mystery novels* (pp. 95–114). New York, NY: Peter Lang Publishing.

Major, C. H. (1998). When power is the limit: The image of the professor in selected fiction. *Innovative Higher Education, 23*(2), 127–143.

Marchalonis, S. (1995). *College girls: A century in fiction.* New Brunswick, NJ: Rutgers University Press.

Marchino, L. A. (1989). The female sleuth in academe. *The Journal of Popular Culture, 23*(3), 89–100.

McChesney, R. W. (1989). Media made sport: A history of sports coverage in the United States. In L. A. Wenner (Ed.), *Media, sports and society* (pp. 49–69). Newberry Park, CA: Sage.

McDermott, M., & Daspit, T. (2005). Vampires on campus: Reflections on (un)death, transformation, and blood knowledges in *The Addiction.* In S. Edgerton, G. Holm, T. Daspit, & P. Farber (Eds.), *Imagining the academy: Higher education and popular culture* (pp. 231–246). New York, NY: RoutledgeFalmer.

McDonough, P. M. (1997). *Choosing colleges: How social class and schools structure opportunity.* Albany, NY: SUNY Press.

Membury, S. (2002). The celluloid archaeologist: An X-rated exposé. In M. Russell (Ed.), *Digging holes in popular culture: Archaeology and science fiction* (pp. 8–18). Oakville, CT: Oxbrow Books.

Messenger, C. K. (1981). *Sport and the spirit of play in American fiction: Hawthorne to Faulkner.* New York, NY: Columbia University Press.

Miller, A. C. (2010). The American dream goes to college: The cinematic student athletes of college football. *The Journal of Popular Culture, 43*(6), 1222–1241.

Mullen, A. L. (2010). *Degrees of inequality: Culture, class, and gender in American higher education.* Baltimore, MD: Johns Hopkins University Press.

Nicol, B. (2011). 'Police thy neighbour': Crime culture and the rear window paradigm. In B. Nicol, P. Pulham, & E. McNulty (Eds.), *Crime culture: Figuring criminality in fiction and film* (pp. 192–209). London, UK: Continuum International Publishing Group.

Owens, T. (2011). Madame Curie above the fold: Divergent perspectives on Curie's visit to the United States in the American press. *Science Communication, 33*(1), 98–119.

Parrott-Sheffer, A. (2008). Not a laughing matter: The portrayals of Black colleges on television. In M. Gasman & C. L. Tudico (Eds.), *Historically Black colleges and universities: Triumphs, troubles, and taboos* (pp. 207–222). New York, NY: Palgrave MacMillan.

Pascarella, E. T., Pierson, C. T., Wolniak, G. C., & Terenzini, P. T. (2004). First generation college students: Additional evidence on college experiences and outcomes. *Journal of Higher Education, 75*(3), 249–284.

Pike, G. R., & Kuh, G. D. (2005). First- and second-generation college students: A comparison of their engagement and intellectual development. *Journal of Higher Education, 76*(3), 276–300.

Pinsker, S. (2003). Postmodernist theory and the academic novel's latest turn. *The Sewanee Review, 111*(1), 183–191.

Pittman, V. V. (1988). Villainy, incompetence, and foolishness: Correspondence study in fiction. *Distance Education, 9*(2), 225–233.

Pittman, V. V. (1992). Outsiders in academe: Night school students in American fiction. *Journal of Continuing Higher Education, 40*(2), 8–13.

Pittman, V. V. (1999). The good, the bad, and the clueless: Night school in the academic mystery. In P. Nover (Ed.), *The great good place? A collection of essays on American and British college mystery novels* (pp. 75–84). New York, NY: Peter Lang Publishing.

Pittman, V. V., & Osborn, R. (2000). Paragons of virtue: World War II veterans in the media of popular culture. *The Journal of Continuing Higher Education, 48*(2), 21–27.

Pittman, V. V., Jr., & Theilmann, J. M. (1986). The administrator in fiction: Portrayals of higher education. *The Educational Forum, 50*(4), 405–418.

Polan, D. (1986). *Power and paranoia: History, narrative, and the American cinema, 1940–1950.* New York, NY: Columbia University Press.

Pope, D. G., & Pope, J. C. (2009). The impact of college sports success on the quantity and quality of student applications. *Southern Economic Journal, 75*(3), 750–780.

Radcliff, M. (2008). Absentminded professor or romantic artist? The depiction of creativity in documentary biographies of Albert Einstein. *Journal of Popular Film and Television, 36*(2), 62–71.

Reynolds, P. J. (2007). *The "reel" professoriate: The portrayal of professors in American film, 1930–1950* (Doctoral dissertation). Indiana University, Bloomington.

Reynolds, P. J. (2009). The celluloid ceiling: Women academics, social values, and narrative in 1940s American film. *Gender and Education, 21*(2), 209–224.

Reynolds, P. J., & Mendez, J. P. (2009, April). *ABC Family's 'Greek': Examining the portrayal of a "real" college experience?* Research paper presented at the annual meeting of the American Educational Research Association (AERA), San Diego, CA.

Reynolds, P. J., & Mendez, J. P. (2012, April). *Flirting, fashion and fun: The gendered portrayal of female college students in ABC Family's 'Greek.'* Research paper presented at the annual meeting of the American Educational Research Association (AERA), Vancouver, British Columbia, Canada.

Richardson, C. (2011). "Can't tell me nothing": Symbolic violence, education, and Kanye West. *Popular Music and Society, 34*(1), 97–112.

Ross, T., Kena, G., Rathbun, A., KewalRamani, A., Zhang, J., Kristapovich, P., & Manning, E. (2012). *Higher education: Gaps in access and persistence study* (NCES 2012-046). U.S. Department of Education, National Center for Education Statistics. Washington, DC: Government Printing Office.

Rudolph, F. (1962/1990). *The American college and university: A history.* Athens: University of Georgia Press.

Russell, C. A., Russell, D. W., & Grube, J. W. (2009). Nature and impact of alcohol messages in a youth-oriented television series. *Journal of Advertising, 38*(3), 97–112.

Ryan, P. A., & Townsend, J. S. (2010). Representations of teachers' and students' inquiry in 1950s television and film. *Educational Studies: A Journal of the American Educational Studies Association, 46*(1), 44–66.

Savada, E. (1995). *The American Film Institute Catalog: Film beginnings, 1893–1910: A work in progress* (Vol. 2). Metuchen, NJ: Scarecrow.

Schwartz, J. (1960). The portrayal of educators in motion pictures, 1950–1958. *Journal of Educational Sociology, 34*(2), 82–90.

Sheppard, R. (1990). From Narragonia to Elysium: Some preliminary reflections on the fictional mage of the academic. In D. Bevan (Ed.), *University fiction* (Vol. 5, pp. 11–48). Atlanta, GA: Rodopi.

Signorielli, N. (2010). Prime-time violence 1993–2001: Has the picture really changed? *Journal of Broadcasting & Electronic Media, 47*(1), 36–57.

Smith, D. R. (2008). Big-time college basketball and the advertising effect: Does success really matter? *Journal of Sports Economics, 9*(4), 387–406. doi:10.1177/1527002507310805

Smith, J. S. (1977). Plucky little ladies and stout-hearted chums: Serial novels for girls, 1900–1920. *Prospects, 3*, 155–174.

Smith, R. A. (2001). *Play-by-play: Radio, television, and big-time college sport.* Baltimore, MD: Johns Hopkins University Press.

Solomon, B. (1985). *In the company of educated women.* New Haven, CT: Yale University Press.

Speed, L. (2001). Moving on up: Education in Black American youth films. *Journal of Popular Film and Television, 29*(2), 82–91.

Steinke, J. (2005). Cultural representations of gender and science: Portrayals of female scientists and engineers in popular films. *Science Communication, 27*(1), 27–63.

Storey, J. (2012). *Cultural theory and popular culture: An introduction.* New York, NY: Routledge.

Studwell, W., & Schueneman, B. (2001). *College fight songs II: A supplementary anthology* (Vol. 2). New York, NY: Haworth Press.

Surber, J. P. (1998). *Culture and critique: An introduction to the critical discourses of cultural studies.* Boulder, CO: Westview Press.

Taylor, A. (1999). The Oxbridge way of death. In P. Nover (Ed.), *The great good place? A collection of essays on American and British college mystery novels* (pp. 15–24). New York, NY: Peter Lang Publishing.

Taylor, L. D. (2005). Effects of visual and verbal sexual television content and perceived realism on attitudes and beliefs. *Journal of Sex Research, 42*(2), 130–137. doi:10.1080/00224490509552266

Terzian, S. G., & Grunzke, A. L. (2007). Scrambled eggheads: Ambivalent representations of scientists in six Hollywood film comedies from 1961 to 1965. *Public Understanding of Science, 16*(4), 407–419.

Thelin, J. R. (2011). *A history of American higher education.* Baltimore, MD: Johns Hopkins University Press.

Thelin, J. R., & Townsend, B. K. (1988). Fiction to fact: College novels and the study of higher education. In J. C. Smart (Ed.), *Higher education: Handbook of theory and research* (Vol. 4, pp. 183–211). New York, NY: Agathon Press.

Tice, K. W. (2005). Queens of academe: Campus pageantry and student life. *Feminist Studies, 31*(2), 250–283.

Tice, K. W. (2012). *Queens of academe: Beauty pageantry, student bodies, and college life.* New York, NY: Oxford University Press.

Tierney, W. G. (2004). Academic freedom and tenure: Between fiction and reality. *The Journal of Higher Education, 75*(2), 161–177.

Tobolowsky, B. F. (2001). *The influence of prime-time television on Latinas' college aspirations and expectations* (Doctoral dissertation). University of California, Los Angeles.

Tobolowsky, B. F. (2006). Beyond demographics: Understanding the college experience through television. In F. S. Laanan (Ed.), *New Directions for Student Services: No. 114. Students in transition: Trends and issues* (pp. 17–26). San Francisco, CA: Jossey-Bass.

Tobolowsky, B. F. (2012, November). *The primetime professoriate: Televisual representations of higher education faculty.* Conference paper presented at the annual meeting of the Association for the study of Higher Education, Las Vegas.

Tobolowsky, B. F., & Lowery, J. W. (2006). Commercializing college: An analysis of college representations during bowl games. *International Journal of Educational Advancement, 6*(3), 232–242.

Toma, J. D., & Cross, M. E. (1998). Intercollegiate athletics and student college choice: Exploring the impact of championship seasons on undergraduate applications. *Research in Higher Education, 39*(6), 633–661.

Toumey, C. P. (1992). The moral character of mad scientists: A cultural critique of science. *Science, Technology, & Human Values, 17*(4), 411–437.

Trier, J. (2003). Inquiring into 'techniques of power' with preservice teachers through the 'school film' *The Paper Chase. Teaching and Teacher Education, 19*(5), 543–557.

Trier, J. (2010). Representations of education in HBO's "The Wire," Season 4. *Teacher Education Weekly, 37*(2), 179–200.

Trow, M. (1999). From mass higher education to universal access: The American advantage. *Minerva, 37*(4), 303–328.

Tucciarone, K. M. (2007a). Cinematic college 'National Lampoon's Animal House' teaches theories of student development. *College Student Journal, 41*, 843–858.

Tucciarone, K. M. (2007b). Community college image—By Hollywood. *Community College Enterprise, 13*(1), 37–53.

Turner, G. (2006). *Film as social practice IV*. New York, NY: Routledge.

Umphlett, W. L. (1984). *The movies go to college: Hollywood and the world of the college-life film.* Madison, NJ: Fairleigh Dickinson University Press.

University of Redlands. (2014). *Freshman survey.* Retrieved from http://www.redlands.edu /news/17109.aspx

Venegas, R. (2012). *Anything but brown: Latino portrayals in higher education films.* Unpublished manuscript.

Villani, S. (2001). Impact of media on children and adolescents: A 10-year review of the research. *Journal of the American Academy of Child & Adolescent Psychiatry, 40*(4), 392–401.

Ward, L. M. (2003). Understanding the role of entertainment media in the sexual socialization of American youth: A review of empirical research. *Developmental Review, 23*(3), 347–388.

Ward, L. M., & Friedman, K. (2006). Using TV as a guide: Associations between television viewing and adolescents' sexual attitudes and behavior. *Journal of Research on Adolescence, 16*(1), 133–156.

Wasylkiw, L., & Currie, M. (2012). The "Animal House" effect: How university-themed comedy films affect students' attitudes. *Social Psychology of Education: An International Journal, 15*(1), 25–40.

Weaver, J. A. (2009). *Popular culture primer.* New York, NY: Peter Lang Publishing.

Weingart, P. (2006). Chemists and their craft in fiction film. *HYLE—International Journal for Philosophy of Chemistry, 12*(1), 31–44.

Weingart, P., Muhl, C., & Pansegrau, P. (2003). Of power maniacs and unethical geniuses: Science and scientists in fiction film. *Public Understanding of Science, 12*(3), 279–287.

Welter, B. (1966). The cult of true womanhood: 1820–1860. *American Quarterly, 18*(2), 151–174.

Wilcox, R. V. (1999). There will never be a "very special" *Buffy: Buffy* and the monsters of teen life. *Journal of Popular Film and Television, 27*(2), 16–23.

Williams, J. J. (2012). The rise of the academic novel. *American Literary History, 24*(3), 561–589.

Winstead, J. L. (2005). *College singing in American college life: 1636–1860* (Doctoral dissertation). University of Georgia, Athens.

Yakaboski, T. (2011). Quietly stripping the pastels: The undergraduate gender gap. *The Review of Higher Education, 34*(4), 555–580.

Yakaboski, T., & Donahoo, S. (2012, March). *Girls in the wild: Representations of student affairs issues affecting college women in Hollywood films.* Presentation at the 2012 NASPA Annual Conference, Phoenix, AZ.

Yang, M., Roskos-Ewoldsen, D. R., Dinu, L., & Arpan, L. M. (2006). The effectiveness of "in-game" advertising: Comparing college students' explicit and implicit memory for brand names. *Journal of Advertising, 35*(4), 143–152.

Young, A. J. K. (2005). "Should I stay or should I go?" Lesbian professors in popular culture. In S. Edgerton, G. Holm, T. Daspit, & P. Farber (Eds.), *Imagining the academy: Higher education and popular culture* (pp. 197–216). New York, NY: RoutledgeFalmer.

Name Index

T

Taylor, A., 33
Taylor, L. D., 2, 4, 110
Terenzini, P. T., 5
Terzian, S. G., 54, 60
Theilmann, J. M., 43, 44, 49
Thelin, J. R., 2, 6, 15, 18, 19, 23, 24, 33, 88
Thomas-Graham, P., 78
Tice, K. W., 37
Tierney, W. G., 30, 59, 64, 66, 68
Tinto, V., 5
Tobolowsky, B. F., 2, 4, 28, 29, 30, 35, 44, 51, 53, 66, 72, 73, 78, 110, 113, 115
Toma, J. D., 110
Toumey, C. P., 57
Townsend, J. S., 75, 103, 104
Trier, J., 57, 59, 63
Trow, M., 23
Tucciarone, K. M., 4, 34, 35, 49, 53, 62, 97, 110
Tunagur, U., 75
Turner, G., 2, 7

U

Umphlett, W. L., 16, 22, 24, 30, 31, 81, 83, 102

V

Venegas, R., 94
Villani, S., 2, 4, 110

W

Ward, L. M., 2, 4, 110
Wartella, E., 1, 110
Wasylkiw, L., 2, 4, 110
Weaver, J. A., 7, 86
Weingart, P., 54, 58, 59
Welter, B., 99
West, K., 16
Wilcox, R. V., 99
Williams, J. J., 17
Williams, R., 3, 62
Winstead, J. L., 14, 23, 24
Wolniak, G. C., 5

Y

Yakaboski, T., 22, 24, 25, 30, 97, 98, 111, 123
Yang, M., 4
Young, A. J. K., 77

Z

Zhang, J., 110

Subject Index

About the Author

Pauline J. Reynolds is an associate professor and program chair for the higher education MA program at the University of Redlands, in Southern California, where she teaches, among other classes, a popular culture and higher education course. Her scholarly interests include examining representations of higher education in popular culture, student and faculty success, and gender in higher education. She holds a BMus (Hons.) from the Royal College of Music, London, England, as well as an MMus and PhD in higher education from Indiana University.

About the ASHE Higher Education Report Series

Since 1983, the ASHE (formerly ASHE-ERIC) Higher Education Report Series has been providing researchers, scholars, and practitioners with timely and substantive information on the critical issues facing higher education. Each monograph presents a definitive analysis of a higher education problem or issue, based on a thorough synthesis of significant literature and institutional experiences. Topics range from planning to diversity and multiculturalism, to performance indicators, to curricular innovations. The mission of the Series is to link the best of higher education research and practice to inform decision making and policy. The reports connect conventional wisdom with research and are designed to help busy individuals keep up with the higher education literature. Authors are scholars and practitioners in the academic community. Each report includes an executive summary, review of the pertinent literature, descriptions of effective educational practices, and a summary of key issues to keep in mind to improve educational policies and practice.

The Series is one of the most peer reviewed in higher education. A National Advisory Board made up of ASHE members reviews proposals. A National Review Board of ASHE scholars and practitioners reviews completed manuscripts. Six monographs are published each year and they are approximately 144 pages in length. The reports are widely disseminated through Jossey-Bass and John Wiley & Sons, and they are available online to subscribing institutions through Wiley Online Library (http://wileyonlinelibrary.com).

Call for Proposals

The ASHE Higher Education Report Series is actively looking for proposals. We encourage you to contact one of the editors, Dr. Kelly Ward (kaward@wsu.edu) or Dr. Lisa Wolf-Wendel (lwolf@ku.edu), with your ideas.

ASHE HIGHER EDUCATION REPORT

ORDER FORM SUBSCRIPTION AND SINGLE ISSUES

DISCOUNTED BACK ISSUES:

Use this form to receive 20% off all back issues of *ASHE Higher Education Report.*
All single issues priced at **$23.20** (normally $29.00)

TITLE   ISSUE NO.   ISBN

_____ _____ _____

_____ _____ _____

_____ _____ _____

*Call 888-378-2537 or see mailing instructions below. When calling, mention the promotional code JBNND
to receive your discount. For a complete list of issues, please visit www.josseybass.com/go/aehe*

SUBSCRIPTIONS: (1 YEAR, 6 ISSUES)

☐ New Order   ☐ Renewal

U.S.	☐ Individual: $174	☐ Institutional: $327
CANADA/MEXICO	☐ Individual: $174	☐ Institutional: $387
ALL OTHERS	☐ Individual: $210	☐ Institutional: $438

Call 888-378-2537 or see mailing and pricing instructions below.
Online subscriptions are available at www.onlinelibrary.wiley.com

ORDER TOTALS:

Issue / Subscription Amount: $ _____

Shipping Amount: $ _____
(for single issues only – subscription prices include shipping)

Total Amount: $ _____

SHIPPING CHARGES:

First Item $6.00
Each Add'l Item $2.00

*(No sales tax for U.S. subscriptions. Canadian residents, add GST for subscription orders. Individual rate subscriptions must
be paid by personal check or credit card. Individual rate subscriptions may not be resold as library copies.)*

BILLING & SHIPPING INFORMATION:

☐ **PAYMENT ENCLOSED:** *(U.S. check or money order only. All payments must be in U.S. dollars.)*

☐ **CREDIT CARD:**   ☐ VISA   ☐ MC   ☐ AMEX

Card number _____Exp. Date_____

Card Holder Name_____Card Issue #_____

Signature _____Day Phone_____

☐ **BILL ME:** *(U.S. institutional orders only. Purchase order required.)*

Purchase order # _____
         Federal Tax ID 13559302 • GST 89102-8052

Name_____

Address_____

Phone_____ E-mail_____

Copy or detach page and send to: **John Wiley & Sons, One Montgomery Street, Suite 1200,
San Francisco, CA 94104-4594**

Order Form can also be faxed to: **888-481-2665**

PROMO JBNND

CPSIA information can be obtained
at www.ICGtesting.com
Printed in the USA
FSOW03n1003230817
37869FS

9 781118 966235